autobiography of
# Robert Flockhart
## THE STREET PREACHER

BAKER BOOK HOUSE
Grand Rapids, Michigan

Paperback edition issued 1977
ISBN: 0-8010-3713-1

PHOTOLITHOPRINTED BY CUSHING - MALLOY, INC.
ANN ARBOR, MICHIGAN, UNITED STATES OF AMERICA
1977

# PREFACE

It was before the fall of the leaf in 1857, but when the fields around Edinburgh, along the foot of the Pentland Hills, and on the shores of the Firth of Forth, were flashing with sickles, and white for the harvest, that Robert Flockhart, the author and subject of the following memoir, fell like a shock of corn in its season.

On the morning of the day that proved to be his last upon earth, I received a letter informing me that he was dying, and that he had expressed a wish to see me. I hastened to his house in Richmond Place. Knowing that his wife was dead, and that he had no child to nurse him in his old age, I feared that I should find him but poorly attended to; but his Master had provided kind friends for the old man's comfort. The small apartment in which he dwelt, and whose walls, if I may say so, he had sanctified by so many prayers, was clean and tidy, and I found a young man and woman watching over him, and ministering to his wants with filial affection. On entering the apartment, I was much struck by his aspect. Propped up for freer breathing, his head lay quietly on a snow-white pillow; and although the film of death was on his eye, and the features were sharp and pinched, his countenance was, as it were, radiant. I have seen many dying ; but none whose face wore an air so heavenly. It looked as if light was streaming on it down from those gates of glory that angel hands were rolling open to admit his departing spirit. They told him that I had arrived. Making an effort, and stretching out his hand, which was burning hot—for by this time he was posting fast to eternity—he said, in a low whisper, and in his own kind and homely way, " O man, I'm glad to see you." Perhaps I should have congratulated him, as one who had been a good soldier of Jesus Christ, and had, through grace, fought the battle well, that his fight was so nearly done, and the crown so nearly won. But having a great regard for him, and great admiration of the large and loving heart, of the self-denying devotedness, and of the true Christian heroism, with which he had served our common Master, I could not help thinking more of our loss than of his gain, and saying that I was sorry to see him laid so low. It would be difficult to convey to the reader any adequate idea of the delight expressed in the look and the tone with which he quickly replied, " I'm going home, I'm going home." The scene was worth a thousand sermons, and would have given birth in the heart of the coldest worldling to the wish, " Let me die the death of the righteous, and let my last end be like his." I saw that he was eager to communicate something. But by this time his voice was sunk to a whisper, and his speech was so thick and faltering, that although I bent over his pillow to catch the words, all that I could gather was something about—"you, and life." One of his attendants explained that he wished to commit to my care a Life of himself, in the hope that I would take charge of it. On my at once assenting to the request, an expression of great satisfaction passed, like a sunbeam, over his dying face, and pressing my hand, he thanked me as best he could.

Having joined together in prayer, or rather in praise and thanksgiving, we parted in the hope of meeting in a better world; and in a very few hours afterwards, the Master he had loved so well and served so long, said, "Come up hither!"

In the following memoir, the reader will find the best portrait of the heart and soul of this remarkable man. Robert Flockhart had been a great sinner, and He who in other days had changed the bitterest persecutor of the church into its noblest preacher, had changed him into a great saint. He had sinned much, had been forgiven much, and so he loved much. He had often exposed himself to disgrace, danger, and death itself in Satan's service; and, if there had been need for it, I believe there was no man in Edinburgh who would have gone to the stake or scaffold for Jesus Christ with a firmer step or nobler bearing than this brave old soldier of the cross. He united the most ardent piety and untiring zeal to indomitable courage, and had no idea of flinching, whether he was called to fight the French at Port Louis, or for Christ and God's truth, face ribald crowds in the High Street or West Port of Edinburgh.

As to his bodily appearance, his presence, like that of Paul's, might be called "contemptible." He was a

man of diminutive stature ; he had a shuffling gait ;
he was ill hung in the limbs ; and had a curious cast
of the eye. On the other hand, his face, reflecting
like a mirror the emotions of the inner man, and every
feeling which swept over his soul, was full of expression.
He abounded in the gesticulations of a natural oratory ;
and being endowed with keen sensibility, and easily
affected himself, he had therefore the power of moving
others.

It must be confessed that he was at times carried
beyond the bounds of propriety by the vehemence of
his feelings. We have read a defence made by a
Highland minister of the sins of his people, which was
certainly more ingenious than sound : He said, that
their vices sprang out of their virtues—they were a
brave people, therefore they were given to fighting and
quarrels—they were by nature very polite, therefore,
to make themselves agreeable, they did not always
stick to the truth—they were very hospitable, therefore
they often got drunk. With more justice I may say,
that Robert Flockhart's defects were the excess of noble
properties. His vehemence in the cause of religion
occasionally ran him into intemperance ; his graphic
powers, although consecrated to God, occasionally passed
from the picturesque into the grotesque ; and having,
like most other men of true genius, a very lively sense
of the ludicrous, he sometimes indulged his humour in
circumstances where it would have been better restrained. There are many stories of smart repartees
and odd sayings fathered upon Flockhart, as on Row-
land Hill and other such men, which I believe are not
true ; but so far as they are so, it is but justice to his

memory to remember the rude and irritating provocations to which, as a street preacher, he was often exposed, and also that he was the foremost to acknowledge his own faults, saying, " I know that I sometimes say what I should not."

The following autobiography was written to dictation, at various times, and by various hands, and the pecuniary profits are to be given to the Indian mission, as Robert Flockhart wished, because it was in India that God called and converted him. It has cost some trouble to put it into shape and order, but in doing so, the editor has been careful to preserve its *salt*, and give it to the church and world, as given to him, with as few alterations as possible. He leaves Robert to speak for himself ; but while admiring the zeal, and powers, and piety of a man who has in so many things set us an example that we should follow him, even as he followed Christ, the editor is not to be understood as approving of everything that he either said or did. He has only further to add, in justice to the memory of two excellent men, who appear, according to the memoir, to have acted harshly towards Flockhart, that he has no doubt, unaccustomed as the world then was to street preaching, and imperfectly acquainted, as they were, with Robert's peculiar temperament, that Dr Stewart and the Rev. Christopher Anderson looked upon him as insane, and one who had no right to say with Paul, " I am not mad, most noble Festus !"

T. G.

EDINBURGH, *March* 31*st* 1858.

# CONTENTS

# Autobiography of Robert Flockhart

## PART I.—BEFORE CONVERSION

AFTER repeated entreaties by a beloved brother in the Lord, I sat down to write an account of my life before I died, that the dealings of God's providence and grace might not be buried with me, but be useful to many after I was gone. Having entered into the sixty-fifth year of my age, I became uneasy in my mind at not leaving behind me a record of what the Lord had done for my soul, that it might be the means of encouraging sinners, and be profitable to his own people. I felt very backward to begin; but, having begun, I will persevere if the Lord is pleased to spare me. I have begun with prayer to the Lord that he would bring to my remembrance what I may have forgotten. May the Lord grant that I may do all with a single eye to his glory, and from a sense of his love to me! May I be enabled to show my love to him by using every means in my power, agreeably to his word, to bring souls to him, not only while I live, but after I am dead!

My father was born in Leith. His parents died when he was young. He was admitted into the West Church Workhouse, and brought up there until he was fit for a trade. He was then taken out and apprenticed to the trade of nail-making in the country, between Edinburgh and Glasgow. After his time was served he came to work in Edinburgh, where he got married to a servant, who became my mother.—My father was then about twenty-three years of age, and my mother eighteen.

Some little time after, they went to Dalnottar, ten miles from Glasgow, where I was born before my mother was nineteen years of age. Dalnottar was a factory for nailers and smiths of various descriptions, employed by Gillis and Company, who sent their work abroad at that time. At that period it might justly have been termed another Sodom. I think there were about a hundred families in the place, and the "fear of God" was not in one of them. In this place (Dalnottar), on the 4th day of February 1778, about half-past three o'clock in the morning, I, Robert Flockhart, was born. Shortly after this, my parents returned to Edinburgh, where they remained till I was ten years of age. I was sent to school when I was five years of age, to one Joseph Robertson, who afterwards became a minister. I remained at his school about five years, when my parents went back again to Dalnottar, and there I served an apprenticeship to the nail-making for seven years. The Lord knows it was a bad place in which to train up the young. I saw no religion nor godly practice all the time I was there. My father made his children learn the Mother's and Shorter Catechisms, and this was all the religious instruction I got whilst I remained with them. There was no explanation given of what I learned, nor any good example set before me. We went next to Greenock, and remained there for nearly a twelvemonth; still "living without God and without hope in the world." All those who do so will "wax worse and worse." This was *my* case.

During the time my parents remained in Greenock, I left them, and went to work in Irvine, where I remained a month. From Irvine I went to Kilmarnock, and there I remained a fortnight, and wrought at my trade in both places, until my mother came from Greenock, and brought home the wanderer. We went next to work in Glasgow; but I was not long there until I enlisted in the Breadalbane Fencibles, who at this time were stationed in Glasgow and Edinburgh. However, as I was below the "standard," being only five feet three inches, they would not keep me. Being rejected by the "Fencibles," I next proceeded to Leith, where I wrought for a short time, but could not rest, as I did not like the trade to which I had served my apprenticeship. On this I consulted with an old soldier as to what I should do. He advised me to enlist in a "regular regiment." He said, if I behaved myself, I might do very well. So I enlisted with a "recruiting" party for a "regular regiment," in the year 1797, about the time the soldiers' pay was advanced from sixpence to a shilling. I then embarked at Newhaven, with some other recruits, for Gravesend, from whence we marched to Chatham. The time we took to sail from Newhaven to Gravesend was a fortnight. On the passage we had very stormy weather, and we thought we should be lost. My bed was either on a coil of ropes or on the deck, and I think I had not my clothes off all the time. When we came to Chatham, we were ordered into a barrack-room; there we met such characters as I had never seen nor heard of before. Nothing but swearing, drinking, quarrelling, and fighting on every hand. I thought they were very wicked men, and did not like to be obliged to live with such characters at first. The body of the 81st regiment had come from the West Indies, sadly thinned by disease and the climate, and they filled it up with recruits, and I was one of them. Our numbers being completed, we embarked for Guernsey. We filled two transports. The one I was in was six weeks in reaching her destination.

The regiment was composed chiefly of Englishmen and Irishmen; there were very few Scotchmen in it. Being a native of Scotland, they made game of me when I spoke my own mother-tongue. On my passage to Guernsey, a sergeant asked me to do something which I did not like. Being a young soldier I refused. On which, with a cane (commonly called a ratan), that he had in his hand, he gave me such a beating as made my young heart ache, and left marks upon my body for many days after. I took this very ill at the time, and regarded it as hard usage, but afterwards I saw that it smartened me up, and, I believe, was the means that Providence employed to keep me from being flogged at the halberts. I never was flogged all the time I was in the army, and that is what very few of the young soldiers could say. They were very strict and severe after we landed at Guernsey—so much so, indeed, that flogging was almost constantly going on every morning. Gin being cheap, undisciplined men made too free with it, and so got themselves often into scrapes, for which they were severely punished. It was no uncommon thing to see ten or twelve men flogged before breakfast.

It happened to be my turn to be at the wheel along with one of the seamen, to help him to turn the helm when going into the harbour, and, in place of two hours, they kept me four. It being very cold at the time, and the wind blowing pretty fresh, the cold went through my body, and I took the ague, and after that the fever. When we landed I was sent to the hospital, and on my way there an Irish recruit asked me what o'clock it was? Having a watch at the time, I took it out and told him the hour. He asked me to let him see it. I did so, and he put it into his watch-pocket (in a joke, as I thought), and went away with it. Being very unwell, I did not like to make any disturbance, and so went to the hospital without my watch. After remaining in the hospital a fortnight, I came out (sooner indeed than I ought to have done) to look after my watch. On asking for it, I was informed by my Irish friend that he had it not. I then asked him where it was ? He replied that he had injured it, and that he had sent it to the watchmaker's to be repaired. I believed him, until I found that he was very long in getting it repaired, when I threatened him, and said I would report him to the captain of the company if he did not bring it back to me the day following. That very night he stole a watch from one of his own countrymen, which, curious to relate, was the cause of my getting back my watch. And the way was this :—His country-man, from whom he had stolen the watch, dis-covered where his property was concealed. He had pawned it, as he had formerly done mine, with a man who kept the barrack-canteen or public-house. The result was, that his country-man " reported " him for stealing his watch ; he denied the charge ; the regiment was ordered to fall in ; the roll was called to see if there were any absent ; the canteen-man, with an officer, went through the ranks and picked him out as the delinquent ; he was then tried and found guilty, and got, I think, five hundred lashes on the bare back. However, I never reported him for taking my watch. Some time after, I inquired at the canteen-man if he (the man who had been flogged) had pawned any other watch with him ; he replied that he had. On which I told him that I had lost mine, and suspected it was the watch he had in his possession, at the same time mentioning the number and maker's name, on which he gave it back to me. This was the beginning of my soldiership, and if I were to enter into all the particulars, I should not be able to finish the history of my privations and sufferings during the eighteen years I was in the army, as well as what I have endured since I came out of it. I will confine myself, therefore, to a few.

We remained at Guernsey nearly twelve months, during which period we were almost constantly on drill or duty. We were expecting the French to land on the island every night, and, in consequence, had provided beacons of dry whins on all the most conspicuous places around. A sentinel was stationed beside each beacon, and his orders were to fire it on the first alarm, so that the inhabitants might be prepared for the enemy. These preparations, however, proved unnecessary, as no landing was attempted. When the year was nearly spent, we got the route to the Cape of Good Hope. We embarked in a large ship named the Coromandel, formerly a 74 gun-ship, but now cut down to a transport. Before she was out of sight of land she struck on a rock, and remained immovable. She then hoisted a flag of distress, and fired signal guns, to apprise the ships in the harbour of her situation ; she was soon surrounded by boats, and by their assistance once more got afloat. After this

we met with no further mishaps till we reached
Spithead. We had formerly occupied six weeks
in sailing from Chatham to Guernsey,—now, we
made the voyage from Guernsey to Spithead in
two days. When we arrived at Spithead, our
regiment was divided among different ships
bound for the Cape of Good Hope. There was a
large fleet of merchant ships (one hundred and
six in number) that sailed with us, bound for
different parts of the world. We had a 98 gun-
ship and two frigates for our convoy, to save us
from being captured by the French. When any
strange sail appeared, the commodore hoisted a
signal to one of the frigates to go and see
whether it was an enemy or a friend. Immediately the frigate would crowd all sail, and flee
like a bird after them, and having got the
required information, bring back word again.
However, we never came in contact with an
enemy of any description during the whole
voyage.

You would have wondered to see the care the
commodore took of all the vessels under his
charge. At one time he would sail slow to keep
them all together, lest the enemy should take
them. At night he would throw up sky-rockets,
and burn blue lights, to make the ships keep
close to him for fear of danger. If an enemy
appeared, he would fight that enemy until he
would go to the bottom, before he would suffer a
single ship under his care to be taken.

I think this resembles the care that Jesus

Christ takes of his fleet sailing to the haven above—(by his fleet, I mean his church)—" lest any hurt it, I will keep it night and day " (Isa. xxvii. 3). "My sheep hear my voice, and I know them, and they follow me: And I give unto them eternal life ; and they shall never perish, neither shall any man pluck them out of my hand. My Father, which gave them me, is greater than all ; and no man is able to pluck them out of my Father's hand" (John x. 27, 28, 29).

During our passage from England to the Cape of Good Hope, out of about one hundred men thirty died. They died very suddenly. Some would be well in the morning, and be dead before night. When dead, the sailors would sew them up in a hammock, with a bag of sand at their feet, and throw them overboard immediately, because they thought the disease of which they died was the plague.

Whenever a storm came on us we expected to go to the bottom, and if we had, many, if not all of us, would have gone to the bottomless pit, and I among the rest. I think the fear of God was not in all the ship. O the amazing patience and long-suffering of God ! Yet, notwithstanding I saw his righteous judgments executed upon others, it never moved me, nor any that I saw ; for, to my shame I acknowledge it, I still waxed worse and worse. Though the Lord's hand was lifted up, I never saw, and though his judgments were abroad, I never learned righteousness, till he

began the work of grace in my heart by his word
and spirit.

We were three months on our passage from
England to the Cape of Good Hope. We arrived
in the month of January 1799. Although the
middle of winter with us, it was the middle of
summer at the Cape. Numbers of our men died
soon after we arrived, and many more during the
time we remained ; for, although the climate is
healthy, and the water good in Cape Town, yet
the immoderate use of cheap wine and cheap fruit,
together with immoral conduct, shortened men's
days. The wicked, as the word of God says,
" shall not live out half his days." I wonder
many a time that the Lord did not cut me off as
well as the rest. It was not because I was better
than they. I ran greedily in the practice and commission of every sin that my wicked heart could
devise, all the time I was there, and that was nearly
four years. I would be ashamed if the world knew
my conduct during this period. How much more
ought I to be ashamed before Him " who is of
purer eyes than to behold iniquity, and who cannot look on sin but with abhorrence ! "

The Sabbath used to be the day on which I
committed most evil, and I gloried in my sin
with my ungodly companions. I felt ashamed
after sinning before I came to the Cape of Good
Hope, but there I lost all shame. Well may I
say, " Wonder, O heavens, be astonished O earth,"
that the Lord should bear so long with such a
wretched sinful man as I was ! I believe that

there is not a sin in the Bible I have not been actually guilty of, except murder. It is true I was restrained from the actual commission of that sin, but I was guilty of it times without number in my heart, for, as the apostle John says, "whosoever hateth his brother is a murderer." I have been convinced, since the Lord has begun a work of grace in my heart by his spirit, that my sins were the cause of Christ's death ; so I acknowledge I am guilty of that murder. I murdered the Holy One and the Just, and that is the worst of all murders.

> " Alas! I knew not what I did,
>   But all my tears are vain !
> Where shall my trembling soul be hid,
>   For I the Lord have slain ? "

Now I can see that, even then, the Lord was kind to me, inasmuch, as in his kind, long-suffering, and gracious providence, he concealed my conduct from the eyes of my superiors, who would have punished me severely had they been made aware of my evil practices. The Lord, however, took that into his own hand, as I shall explain afterwards. I have also been often exposed to hungry wild beasts during the night, when on duty at my post, and I had nothing to defend me but God's providence.

In the year 1803, all the regiments got orders from the government at home to leave the Cape, it being given over to the Dutch at that time. The 81st regiment (which I belonged to), and the 91st, were ordered to come to England ; but the 8th dragoons and the 22d were to go to Bengal,

and the 65th either to Madras or Bombay.   Any
man, however, belonging to the two regiments
that were ordered home, was at liberty to volunteer into any of the three regiments that were
going abroad, and get two guineas of volunteer
money.   I think there were three days given
for the volunteering.   On the first day, a great
many of my comrades volunteered, and got their
bounty money.   I had been thinking of coming
home along with the 81st, and the subject had
taken such a strong hold of my mind as to deprive
me of sleep for nearly a whole night before I
could come to a decision.   As I lay on my bed,
I reasoned thus with myself : If I go home,
what have I made by being abroad ?   After all
my sufferings and privations, I am just as poor as
when I left home.   These reflections decided me,
and I resolved to volunteer into the 22d regiment
the second day.   Since I have come to know the
Lord, I see and acknowledge the over-ruling hand
of his providence in this decision.   Had I gone
home at that time, there was nothing but confusion and war, whilst in India there was time to
read and think, and the Lord sent his servants to
preach to us, if we chose to hear.

We embarked for Calcutta, in Bengal, in the
end of the year 1803.   We were four months on
our passage ; and during that time we often expected to be lost.   One time the ship took fire
near the magazine where the powder was, and we
had great difficulty in getting it put out.   The
magazine was at the stern of the ship, and the

way that it took fire was this : The ship's steward
went into the steerage with a lighted candle, and
the ship, no doubt rocking at the time, the candle
came in contact with the small twigs of some
besoms used for sweeping the ship, but unknown
to him. The fire had been burning for some
time, and as there was only a thin partition of
wood between it and the magazine of gunpowder,
the ship might have been blown up in an instant,
and we might all have been launched into the
presence of God in a moment, and received our
awful doom for ever, but for the kind providence
of God that caused a lady in the cabin to smell
the burning. She gave the alarm that the ship
was on fire ; then every soldier was ordered to
take his blanket out of his hammock, and after
dipping it in the sea by means of a rope that was
tied to it, to throw it on the flames.

By these means they got the fire out, and
blessed be the Lord for that escape also. The
reason I said *they* got the fire out, and not *we*, was
because I had no hand in putting it out. I will
shew the state of my mind at the time, and then
you will know what a selfish, presumptuous,
hardened sinner I was. I said within myself, " I
will not wet my blanket, for there are plenty to
extinguish the fire without me. I will go to the
fore part of the ship, and if the ship be blown up
I will not be killed ; my life will be spared, for I
will throw myself on a plank of the ship until
some vessel pick me up."

I observed that every one was busy, using every

means in his power to put out the fire, excepting
a sailor who was fishing at the bows of the ship,
and had caught a young bottle-nosed porpoise,
with which we were both diverting ourselves
when there was but a thin plank to prevent our
bodies from becoming food for the fishes, and our
souls from being driven out of this world with fire,
into that place where "their worm dieth not, and
the fire is never quenched." O what a contrast
here, when I think of the goodness of God in
Christ to me, notwithstanding the hardness of my
impenitent and rebellious heart towards him ! It
should make me ashamed, and humble me in the
dust before him every time I review my life !

But I feel uneasy in my mind until I go back
to the Cape of Good Hope, to relate some bad
conduct that I was there guilty of.

There were numbers of Irishmen in the 81st
regiment who combined themselves together to
commit rebellion against their lawful sovereign,
then King George the Third. They did not take
the advice that John the Baptist gave to the
soldiers in his days, "to be content with their
wages, and to do violence to no man." They
were not content with their condition, and they intended "violence." They got me to join with
them. One of them was a shoemaker : his name
was Flinn. He was the ringleader. He told me
what they intended to do, and without considering the consequences, I was induced to swear on a
Bible, and kiss that blessed book, that I would be
true to them. He, and some more of his recruits,

were spreading disaffection through the regiment. They complained of little pay, and bad provisions, and they were to do great exploits. One of these was to take possession of the castle, and have the whole Cape to themselves. I was always in company with them drinking. I had, however, but little to say. Give me a glass of wine, that was all I minded ; and it was well for me that the Lord, in his kind providence, shut my mouth, as you will see by what I have to say.

One day Flinn, the ringleader, asked me to go to the canteen to drink some wine with him, and I accordingly went. At that time the 81st and 91st were quartered in the barracks, near the castle. The canteen is a public-house within the barrack-walls for soldiers. Well, you will see how wonderfully God, in his providence, stopped this mutiny in time, by this event. Blessed be his name ! There happened to be one of the 91st at the canteen, and Flinn told him all about what they intended to do. As I stated before, however, my mouth was still dumb on that subject, although I knew all about it. The 91st man being a Scotchman, I used to speak to him about Scotland, for I had a particular great regard for Scotchmen abroad. The 91st man pretended to join with Flinn, and to spread the mutiny through his own regiment. Instead, however, of doing so, he went to a drill-sergeant of his own regiment, and told him all the secret. On which the sergeant disguised himself, and put on a private's coat, and came to a public-house outside the walls of the barracks, and got Flinn to come and explain to him all about the intended mutiny, pretending, at the same time, to join heartily in his project. I happened to be there at the same time, but Flinn did not tell him before me, and the sergeant thought, in consequence of this, that I knew nothing of the matter. I may mention that Flinn went out for some time, and left only him and me together, and he (the sergeant) never spoke a word to me about it, nor I to him. It was in Flinn's absence that I was mysteriously led, in an unusual rapture, to converse about Edinburgh, as he knew about it, until Flinn came in again. I have wondered many a time since that I was so mysteriously restrained from saying one word to the sergeant about the matter which had brought him to visit Flinn, as I am naturally open-minded, and of a free turn, and unsuspicious. I see the over-ruling hand of God's providence in this also.

On the day on which it was Flinn's turn to mount guard, he got leave for me to take his place, promising at the same time to take mine in turn. I see the hand of the Lord in this also. For had I not been on guard, I might have been with the mutineers.

By this time the sergeant had got acquainted with the mutineers' intentions, and had reported them to the officers. I think there were about four or five of this rebellious band, that had agreed to go down to the castle to see the guns, but the sergeant knowing this the night before, had informed the officers of what was contemplated, and when they reached the castle, they were instantly seized and imprisoned. Then a search was made in their knapsacks for papers relating to the plot. I rather think they found none, and it was well for me they did not, for my name might have been found enrolled among them.

After they were some time in prison, word was sent to me from the prisoners to bring in one of their knapsacks, which I did. I had the hardihood to conceal a bottle of wine in the knapsack, and got it brought into the prison in safety, as the keeper of the prison providentially did not open the knapsack, although it was his duty to do so. Although no one was allowed to speak to the prisoners, and sentinels were placed around the prison, I went and watched an opportunity, and got a letter from one of them out of the window to carry to one of their associates. After I got the letter into my possession, a horror seized my mind for the first time, that, if that letter were found upon me, I should be treated as one of their accomplices. I did not therefore deliver it. But I would have given anything to have got into some secret place where I could tear it into small pieces, which I think I did at last. Whilst I had it in my possession, I thought every person would see me. O how glad was I when it was destroyed! I never thought, however, that the Lord saw me. After that I never went near them, until I was ordered to attend as a witness for Flinn at a general court-martial. I went accordingly when it was his turn to be tried, and to my shame, I confess, I took a false oath, for I swore I would tell all I knew, which, if I had done, I would have brought in myself.

There were two witnesses against Flinn, as I mentioned before. The first was the private of the 91st that Flinn and I were drinking with in the canteen, but fortunately I had paid little attention to what they said, as a kind providence directed my attention to a Scotchman, who was amusing the company by whistling through his throat like a bird.

The general court-martial was ordered to be held in the castle. The prisoners and witnesses were brought to the same place. Flinn, the ring-leader, was first tried, and it went greatly against him, until I was brought forward as a witness on his behalf. I think I had heard some men of the 81st regiment, which I then belonged to, say, that the private of the 91st, whose name was Lever, had been guilty of many crimes in his own regiment, and that they had seen his name posted on the gate of the barracks (which I may observe are walled in), so that the sentinel should not let him out. Now, when I was called in as a witness for Flinn, the officers asked me " when it was I met them in the canteen, and my reason for not speaking to Lever, the private of the 91st ?" I replied, " that I did not think it worth while to speak to him, because I saw his name on the gate as one not to be permitted to go out of the barracks." This reply caused them to look

into his character, and it was found not to be very
good. I think this shook their confidence in his
testimony against Flinn. Then they began to
look into my character, and they cross-questioned
me, and it was with much ado I escaped out of
the net. It was greatly in my favour that I had
a good character as a clean soldier, and regular in
every duty, and that I never had been in the
guard-house as a prisoner. O how heedless and
thoughtless was I to rush into such dangers, not
knowing the awful consequences which generally
attend such conduct! Agreeably to the articles
of war, we were all guilty of death. Upon reflection, I feel ashamed of being guilty of such
foolish conduct in making an attempt it was impossible to accomplish.

I believe that Satan lays many snares to ruin
precious souls. I often, when confessing this before God, acknowledge that I deserve to be driven
out of this world with shame, from among men,
into that place where there is nothing but shame
and everlasting contempt. It is of the Lord's
mercies that this has not been the case long before
now. O that I could warn every soldier in the
army against such conduct ; no good can attend
it, but much evil!

The next prisoner that was tried was one George
Anderson, and I was sent for as a witness for him.
I would not go, because having nearly entangled
me the first time, I took good care they should
not do so the second.

The next to be tried was M'Farlane, and I think

there was only another, whose name was Flood Troy. These being found guilty, Flinn was sentenced to be banished to Botany Bay (I cannot tell whether it was for life or for a limited period), and the rest to be flogged. I think Anderson got seven hundred lashes on his naked shoulders, and M'Farlane five hundred. I do not remember whether Flood Troy was punished or not, as I was not present at the place of punishment, being on some other duty at that time. And as to Flinn, he had not been long banished until I saw him in the Cape of Good Hope again, in sailor's dress, free from the army, and free from banishment!

Whoever may read this may probably be wearied with the long detail I have now given. But I saw when I began it, that it would be wrong in me not to tell the whole that I knew about it. Well, if I was not found out by man, and punished by man, the Lord has since that taken me in hands, and has made that, as well as my other sins, bitter to me, by showing me his displeasure against my conduct. However, it has all been in love to my soul. I have learned that although the Lord forgives the sinner through the finished work of his incarnate Son, he takes "vengeance on their inventions." I wonder many a time what possessed me to join such a crew. I was not dissatisfied with my condition, and did not feel revengeful. Bad company, bad counsels, and not considering what the consequences would be, exposed me, a stupid, thoughtless, easy-led young man, to punishment in this world, and everlasting punishment hereafter. I hope that young men will beware of bad company.

Many things that happened during the time we remained in the Cape of Good Hope have escaped my memory. I hope, therefore, excuse will be made for the confused way I have written. All that I have written, or shall write, depends upon the Lord, as he brings it to my remembrance, for I never wrote before, and I am now entered on the 65th year of my age.

I should have mentioned at the beginning, that one time some men of the company I belonged to, and my companions in sin, stole a cask of wine from a Dutchman, and carried it into the fields among bushes, at a station where we lay, called Wineburg. They told me of it, and I went with them and helped them to drink it. It was not discovered who had taken it, else, if it had, we should have been severely punished as thieves, and there was no mercy shown to thieves in the 81st regiment.

At another time a party had agreed to go and steal grapes out of a field at night, and would not take me with them. They thought I could not run so fast as they could, and that if they were chased I should be taken. But I partook and ate of the stolen fruit along with them. So I was like Adam. Eve stole the forbidden fruit, and Adam partook of it. So we see he was equally guilty with her, and exposed himself, and all his posterity, to the same punishment.

At another time there was a great storm. There

were many ships lying in Table Bay at the time. The wind blew a heavy sea into the bay, and anchorage is very bad there in stormy weather. Their anchors began to drag in the middle of the day, and they that followed the example of those that were in Paul's ship escaped. They hoisted up the main-sail, and made towards shore, and got high up upon the beach, and got off again at spring-tide. They knew where to run ashore, and ran their vessels on sandy ground. There was, however, an East Indiaman (I think they called her the "Old Sceptre"), that had been a 94 gun-ship cut down for the East India trade (as I was informed), and she kept her anchors during the day, employing some of the large guns fastened to their cables to hold her fast. They succeeded till the middle of the night, or early in the morning, when she was driven from her moorings upon the rocks, and became a total wreck. When the drum beat to arms, a great number of the soldiers went down to the shore to render assistance. Some made fires on the beach, others plunged into the sea to save the lives of the ship's crew, who were driven about with the violence of the waves amid the timbers of the wreck. Although I was not there (being otherwise engaged, having, if I recollect aright, at that time to mount guard), I was informed that, with great difficulty, they brought fifty alive to shore. All the rest, to the amount of three hundred, perished in the waters !

When it was daylight I went down to the shore, before going on guard, to see the wreck.

A number of dead bodies were lying on the beach. Some were so mangled with the broken timbers whilst in the sea that they could not be carried to the churchyard. A large hole was therefore dug in the sand, into which they were hurriedly thrown and covered up. The rest of the bodies were carried in wagons to Amsterdam churchyard, and there interred. At this time I was on guard, and it happened to be the Navy-hospital guard, which is near the burying-ground. And as the wagoners did not know where the burying-ground was, I was the person who led them to the place.

There I saw a large, deep hole dug. The dead were then taken out of the wagons and laid on the ground in their wet clothes. The sailors that had been saved alive and were able to come from the Navy-hospital, to which they had been sent, were there. Before the dead were thrown into the afore-mentioned hole, one on the top of the other, I saw the living sailors go to them and search their pockets, saying, "This was my mess-mate, and I will take what is here!" They then threw them in, as I have said. But there were seven officers of the ship that had been drowned, who were carried to the guard-house in their clothes, and laid on the guard-bed until coffins had been made for them.

It is remarkable that the storm ceased when the work of death was over, and about three hundred souls launched all at once into eternity. I will now show you that I was as hardened as the rest at this time. To judge from our conduct we were worse than the barbarous people of Melita, for the soldiers that went down to save the people that were drowning were plundering at the time, opening casks of rum and drinking it, and carrying off shirts and other wearables, as well as provisions. As usual, they brought some to me, and I partook of them with great pleasure at that time. I think that was the chief thing that took me down to the beach before I went on guard.

I slept that night on the guard-bed, beside the corpses of the drowned officers, and I felt my mind no more impressed than if I had been lying beside my living comrade! O the hardening nature of sin! No judgments had the least impression on me at that time. I lived as if I had no account to give of my conduct. My ways and doings were so bad at that time that I feel ashamed to speak of them.

There was a company of the 81st regiment sent to do duty about sixteen miles from Cape Town. To this company I belonged. One of the party was entrusted with the care of the sheep intended for our provisions, and he stole one of them, and a few of us boiled it, and I was one of them who helped to eat it in the Navy-hospital guard-houses.

There was at that place a bakehouse where biscuit was made for the navy. They stored the biscuit in a room above the guard-house, and there happened to be a hole in the floor that you might put your hand in. I took biscuit by putting my hand into this hole, as did also many of the rest of my comrades. At last they began to

miss them, and having set a watch, caught a
soldier of another regiment, who was reported to
the colonel, tried by a garrison court-martial,
found guilty, and flogged in the barrack-square
before all the regiments then lying in Cape Town.
This was in the year 1802, when there was likely
to be a famine. In consequence of the threatened
scarcity, both officers and men were put on low
diet. I think twelve ounces of coarse bread and
half a pound of meat was a day's allowance, and
it being a place exposed to the fresh sea-breeze,
and the men all young and healthy, some would
eat all their allowance at one meal. Well, this
young man cried out when they were flogging
him, "O will you not forgive me, and take me
down! Hunger will break through a stone wall."
I felt what he said, for I have often gone to my
bed with a hungry belly and an empty stomach,
and I would think of my father's house, and I
would burst into tears in secret (but not before
my Heavenly Father at that time), but merely
from the pinching hunger that I felt then and
there in a foreign land. It was not so in my
father's house. Many a wistful look I gave to
my earthly father's house, and if I had had wings
I would have flown home at that time.

Although all this was the case, still there is no
allowance for man to steal. If stealing be hateful
in the sight of man, what must it be in the sight
of God? We have many proofs in the Bible of
God's displeasure against this sin. We see it in
the case of Achan's trespass at Jericho. It is

forbidden likewise throughout the Scriptures. It is recorded in the eighth commandment, "Thou shalt not steal." We may make many excuses for doing evil, but at the day of judgment not a shred of excuse will be taken. In the sixth chapter of 1st Corinthians, 9th and 10th verses inclusive, the characters are described that shall not enter into the kingdom of God, living and dying in the indulgence and practice of any of these sins:—"Be not deceived ; neither fornicators, nor idolators, nor adulterers, nor effeminate, nor abusers of themselves with mankind, nor thieves, nor covetous, nor drunkards, nor revilers, nor extortioners, shall inherit the kingdom of God." The church at Corinth had been guilty of such sins, and of some of them in an especial degree. Through the preaching of the gospel by Paul, however, and the blessing of the Lord upon His own word, it came in such power, and in the Holy Ghost, and much assurance, that the Corinthians were brought to repent of all these sins ; for we see in the next verse that they believed in the Lord Jesus Christ, and were washed, and sanctified, and justified.

But as Paul brought the sins of the Corinthians to their remembrance, so I desire to do the same, and I will therefore go on with my story.

One night after evening parade, a number of the soldiers went to take a walk in Cape Town, and I was with them. When it began to be dark, one of the company went away a little distance from us, and never said what he was going to be about. A little after I saw him running as fast as he could, and I called him by his name. When I got to the barracks, I found he was very angry with me for mentioning his name, which was John Smith. He was a native of the north of Ireland. I understood that he had been robbing, or going to rob a Dutchman, and he thought they were pursuing hard after him; but I did not see them, and heard no more about it. If it had been found out, we might both have been executed, as I was in company with him.

Whilst I was in the Cape, Maguire, the man whom I mentioned in the beginning of this narrative, as having carried off my watch and stolen another in Guernsey, for which he was severely flogged, came, much the worse of drink, into the berth that I occupied. He threw himself alongside of my comrade, Hughes, who was a countryman of his own, from Dublin, and told him that he had robbed a Dutchman. While he lay there, the purse that he had stolen fell out of his pocket, and, being drunk, he did not miss it till the morning. My neighbour picked it up, and found that there were eight gold pieces in it, each of which was value for eight shillings. This money I helped my companion to spend in drink. Maguire continued to steal until the Colonel became tired of flogging him, and he got him exchanged for another man out of the 8th Dragoons, who lay at the Cape at that time. However, he was not long with them until he and two of the 81st had made it up that they would try, without it being known, to remain out of quarters all night. They did so accordingly, and went through part of the town, and were engaged in the act of robbing a master printer, when they were apprehended by the patrol. They were confined, and afterwards tried by a general court-martial, and found guilty, and sentenced to be hanged. When their sentence was going to be put in execution, one of them, an Englishman, whose name was Brown, got a pardon at the foot of the ladder. The other two, whose names were Maguire and Callaghan, Irishmen, were executed. Callaghan, when on the ladder, implored mercy from General Dundas, the commander-in-chief, with a cry so lamentable that it affected the hearts of many of the soldiers who were present. But no mercy was given. The other man, Maguire, never said a word. Brown got his pardon when in his dead-clothes, and the rope about his neck. He afterwards got back his regimentals, and was sent to do duty again in his own regiment.

I remember after this, on a field-day, it happened that Brown was next to me in the ranks, and we both marched over the graves of the two men that suffered. Brown looked me in the face and said—"I deserve to be there, for I was as guilty as they were." I have thought since that I may take up the same words when I look back upon my past life, and look down to hell, for I deserve to be there, for I have been as bad, and a great deal worse, than many that are there. O

that I may never forget the sovereign love of God
in Christ to me, the chief of sinners !

Although I was worse than I have words to call
myself, I was always respected in the army. My
wickedness was hid from the eyes of my superiors.
I was like the master I served—subtile. But my
ways and doings were not hid from God. I looked
to men to please them, and get their esteem, and
escape being flogged ; but God was not in all my
thoughts. I practised iniquity with greediness in
secret, and in public without shame, and times
without number, and yet my officers never found
me out but once, which I will relate afterwards.

There were some officers that came to join different regiments that lay at the Cape of Good
Hope. Two of them quarrelled on their passage,
and they were to decide their difference when
they landed. One of them, whose name was
Mackay, belonged to the 91st regiment. The
name of the other was Monteith, and he belonged
to the 81st regiment. They carried out their intentions. Lieutenant Mackay's ball went in
below the right arm of Ensign Monteith. He
lived for about a fortnight after receiving the
wound ; and I was chosen by the captain of the
company as a fit person to attend him, which I
did until he died. I was always ready with a
basin when he coughed, for he spat blood, and on
that account I got another person to assist me,
and then we took the watching turn about. I
remember one time I got him out of bed, and
propped him up with pillows in a chair, when

suddenly he gave a cough, and his heart's blood
came out of his mouth into the basin in my hand.
The last words I heard him say were, "O Lord,
I'm gone," on which he expired, and I burst into
tears.    My assistant told my companions in the
company that I cried at his death, and they
laughed me to scorn.    We will now see the de-
ceitfulness of the heart.    The deceased left a Bible;
I had none.    Well, I told the officer, whose name
was Captain Maclaren, who took charge of all the
deceased left, that the deceased ordered me to get
the Bible when he died, though he never said
such a word.    Now this was coveting God's truth
with a lie.    I got the Bible, and was thus guilty
of covetousness and falsehood, both of which it
condemns.

You see from the conduct of soldiers in our
cities, and even when they are at home, that
they are chiefly guilty of three heinous sins—the
first, drunkenness ; the second, swearing ; and the
third, the worst of all the three, the defiling of
both soul and body.    All other sins are without
the body, but uncleanness is against the body.
This is generally their conduct wherever they go.
But you see nothing at home like what you see
abroad.    Soldiers are restrained here by the presence of their friends, and those who know them,
as well as by the police.    But abroad all restraint
is entirely cast off.    I feel greatly ashamed when
I remember that I myself am the very man that
was guilty of the three heinous sins just mentioned,
and that I went to such a length as to cast off all

shame. I was worse than a beast. I would be ashamed to speak of those things I did in secret, particularly when in the Cape of Good Hope and in the East Indies. The language of my heart was that of the first verse of the fourteenth Psalm—"The fool hath said in his heart that there is no God." I wonder often at the long-suffering and patience of God with me above many. Surely there never was a greater sinner than I have been. I have read John Bunyan's life, but he was nothing to me. It is of the Lord's mercies that I was not swept away in my sins, along with many of my ungodly companions who are now in hell. Perhaps they are now cursing me for my bad conduct along with them, and in helping them to that place where "their worm dieth not, and the fire is never quenched." Many of them died in their sins, and of all such Jesus says, "Where I am, thither ye cannot come." Heaven is the place where he is, and if any one of Adam's fallen race dies in his sins, he cannot get there ; and if he cannot go there, there is but one other place, and that is hell. But we are saved from that by believing that "Jesus Christ is the Son of God," and that he "suffered for our sins, the just for the unjust, that he might bring us to God."

At first, when I went into the army, I was surprised to see in Chatham soldiers' wives washing and dressing men's shirts on the Lord's day. And again, in Guernsey, still more, to see men drinking, and swearing, and fighting on the Sabbath. At the Cape of Good Hope it was still

worse.    There I saw men, not only drinking,
swearing, and fighting, but even singing profane
songs, and working all manner of uncleanness
with greediness, especially on the Lord's day.
Likewise, I saw them gambling at cards, and at
pitch-and-toss.    I was startled at this at first, not
from any love that I had in my heart to holiness,
and hatred to sin, but from my being brought up
in Scotland.    I may well blush and be ashamed
when I speak, or think, or write about these
things, and reflect that I am the very dog that
was guilty of all these sins that I have named, and
of many others that I would not name.

The fact I most deplore in connection with the
army is the immorality of which our men are
guilty abroad.    I know that if a soldier has not
grace in his heart, he is, in a very little time, led
by his fellow-soldiers into every excess of lewd-
ness and profanity.    Even though he has a good
outward moral character at first, " evil commu-
nications" will soon " corrupt good manners."
There can be no hypocrite in the army for any
considerable length of time, for if any soldier makes
a profession of Christianity, that profession will
soon be tried by hot persecution.    But when a
man is tried, and is enabled by the grace of God
to stand fast, and to act consistently with his
Christian profession, he is esteemed even by the
most ungodly.    I know this to be true.

In my writing about the Cape, I was wanting
too soon to be done with it.    But although it be
painful to me, I must go back.    One reason of

my anxiety to be done with it was, that I felt
ashamed that any one should know the ungodly
practices I had been guilty of whilst residing in
it. I considered, however, that I should be much
more ashamed before him who is of purer eyes
than to behold iniquity, and who, where I see
one sin, beholds a thousand. Man sees only the
" outward appearance," but " God sees the heart."
" All things are naked and open unto the eyes of
him with whom we have to do." And he who
is a present witness of all that we do now, will
soon be our impartial judge. We may hide ourselves now, like Adam, " among the trees of the
garden," and cover ourselves with " fig-leaves,"
and think, that because we are respectable among
our own fellow-men, and because we have an outward profession, that all is safe for eternity. But
in the day of judgment there will be no disguise.
We have " sinned against the Lord," and if we do
not find our sin out here, that we may bring it to
the cross of Christ, and look on him whom these
very sins have pierced, until our hearts are melted
into penitential and godly sorrow for all that we
have done, we may be very sure that our sins will
find us out there. O that the Lord would make us
all faithful to ourselves whilst the door of mercy
is open, and save us from covering our sins, for
" He that covereth his sins shall not prosper ;
but whoso confesseth and forsaketh them shall
have mercy " (Prov. xxviii. 13). We may say we
believe, but have we repented ? — the evidence
that I believe is, that I have repented. God

hath joined the two together, and "let no man put them asunder." Believe and be saved; repent and be forgiven.

I mentioned before that our passage from the Cape to Calcutta occupied about four months. I do not remember of any deaths during the voyage. All on board were quite healthy. As our passage was tedious, we ran short of wood and water, and had no fire to cook our meat with for a fortnight. We had therefore to anchor at a place not very far from land, and send a boat on shore for wood and water. The natives, however, would not let us have any either for love or money. Under these circumstances, we contrived to get their king on board the ship, and then made him a present of a watch, of which he was very proud.

While the king was on board, a large party was sent on shore with axes and saws to cut down wood, and with large casks to hold water. We were to take these by force. A guard of soldiers was sent with arms and accoutrements, and I happened to be one of the number. As soon as we landed, we got orders to "prime and load." We were afterwards placed as sentinels to protect the wood and water party, until we got a sufficient quantity of these necessaries. My post was on the beach, to prevent the natives from taking the boat. They were far more numerous than we were, and we could not have succeeded if we had not had their king on board.

After returning on board, a large ship pursued us for a good while. The officers of the ship thought that it was a pirate. We escaped by sailing near the land. The pirate, being a larger ship than ours, could not sail in low water as we did. So she left us, and we at last anchored in Diamond Harbour.

I may remark, that large ships cannot come nearer to Calcutta than Diamond Harbour. It is here that the river Ganges and the sea meet. There were boats ready when we arrived to receive the king's troops, and to bring us up the Ganges to Fort-William, which is at a considerable distance from Diamond Harbour. These boats are covered over like a house, to keep us from the sun. The Honourable Company sent us plenty of fresh provisions, and everything that was for our comfort. At that time private soldiers were treated in India as if they had been officers.

We disembarked a little way from Fort-William. I was in good health when I landed, and it is remarkable, that as soon as I put my foot upon Indian ground, both my knees went to the ground on stepping out of the boat. It was about six years after this that I was brought in reality to bend before a throne of grace, and to cry, with prayers and tears, for mercy. There is nothing new unto God. He knows the end from the beginning. Although the Lord, for ends only known to himself, left me to the will of my own lusts, yet he was determined to save.

However, after all the dangers the Lord delivered me from, whilst bringing me in health and strength safe to land, I never thought upon his goodness. I repaid that with ingratitude, and still went on in my trespasses, adding sin to sin ; "drunkenness unto thirst ; " one unclean and base action to another, until I polluted both soul and body, and at last brought myself to be incapable of doing duty. I was then sent to the hospital, and remained there for six months. During the time I was there, the soldiers were dying every day, and sometimes a great many every day.

One morning I went into the room where they bring the corpse when the breath leaves the body, to be inspected by the doctors. O what a number of naked bodies, that had been newly opened. I could compare it to nothing but the shop of a butcher. All this, however, never moved me. There were deaths on each side of my bed. One of my companions in sin died in my arms, whilst I was lifting him up. But all this made no deep nor lasting impression on my mind ; for when I got well, and came out of the hospital, I joined my old companions in sin, and in place of becoming better, to my shame I confess it, I grew more hardened, and my "heart was fully set," and more bold in the practice of every sin in me to evil. Although the men were still dying very suddenly, it never moved me. The names of the men of every company are alphabetically written down in a roll. I observed that the man before me and the man after me in the roll died. Still, all that never moved me from my old practices. Oh, the hardness and desperate wickedness of my heart! It was seen in my ungodly life

I had the worst men in the company which I belonged to for associates. We used to try who would be foremost in intemperance, filthy conversation, and every evil practice ; and we gloried in it. I wonder that the earth did not open, and swallow me and my ungodly companions up alive, or that, amid the dreadful storms of thunder and lightning, so common in Bengal, God did not sweep me away from the face of the earth, with all my sins about me, into hell, and make me as miserable as I had made myself sinful. In place of that, the Lord was kind to me, giving me health, and sparing my life, and delivering me from many dangers and diseases that took almost all my ungodly companions away. O the long-suffering patience of God in Christ to me above thousands ! I had been perhaps the very worst, and to my shame, I tried to weary out his patience, and abuse the bounties of his providence, making them weapons of rebellion against him, my best and kindest Friend ! This shows the aggravated nature and exceeding sinfulness of my sin. I have no words to describe it. But to proceed.

Whilst we were in Fort-William, war broke out ; first, I think, at a distance of about one hundred miles from us. A part of our regiment, with some regiments of the native soldiers, and a number of artillery with their guns, proceeded to the seat of war, and laid siege to a fort. Whilst they were besieging this fort, and the soldiers at night were sleeping on the ground, the tigers on one occasion came among them, and, seizing one of the sepoys, threw him upon his back, and ran away with him alive for his prey. He lay alongside a white man, at the same time, beside the guns. In the same place our men saw the Hindoos going to burn a living woman with her dead husband, and they took her away by force from a great multitude that was assembled to perform and witness that awful invention, which has long been practised in India. After conquering their enemies, they brought the woman down with them to the regiment, and, as I am informed, they made her a cook.

The second war that broke out was at a place which is called Bhurtpore; I think it is about a thousand miles from Fort-William. General Lake was there besieging a strong fort with a number of regiments, when two of the flank companies of the 22d regiment were called for to go and assist them. Each company consisted of one hundred strong, clever young men, the picked men of the regiment. They were all killed except about seventy, and the most of the seventy were dreadfully wounded. The fort, however, was not conquered ; they sent a flag of truce, and came to terms of peace.

The next war was with a noted robber, who had a great army, all mounted on horseback. His name was Holkar. All the troops were sent on an expedition to pursue after him. This called the whole of the regiment that I was in to leave Fort-William. Fort-William is a large fort about three miles from the city of Calcutta, with port-holes, mounting nearly one thousand guns, and round about it a deep trench to hold water. But before I leave Fort-William I have the best news to tell. The Lord sent his servants from Calcutta to preach the gospel to their countrymen in the 22d regiment, during the time we lay there. Some of the Baptist missionaries, accompanied by a schoolmaster, came privately, and without being sent for. The officers gave orders against it, but this only made them the more desirous to come, and the soldiers the more desirous to hear. Before the missionaries came, I do not think that there was a spark of grace in any man's heart in all the regiment. There was not so much as a mere profession ; and I heard one of the soldiers say, long after (for I would not go amongst them then, I was so busy with the devil's servants in the devil's work), "that the Lord honoured that humble schoolmaster in kindling a fire in the 22d regiment, that all the devils in hell would not put out."

That man, I trust, was converted himself, and he and a few more formed themselves into a church, assembling together, and exhorting one another from the word of God, praying with and for one another, and singing the praises of God. They used to meet for worship every day. This is the way that the fire was kept in which the Lord kindled by the instrumentality of a humble schoolmaster, who volunteered his labour of love among soldiers, and had no earthly reward.

We remained in **Fort-William** about twelve

months. At the end of that period we left it. We crossed the Ganges a little way from Calcutta to the other side, at a place called "Sulkyside," and then marched up the country. We had not gone far until we came to a place called "Monkey Wood." Here there is a grove of trees covered with large monkeys, which the people all round about flock to worship and feed. We had strict orders not to touch one of them, for the natives there held them sacred. Had we hurt any of them the whole of the inhabitants would have risen against us. The monkeys were very tame.

We came next to a place called Allahabad, where there is a garrison of European invalids that belong to the Honourable Company's service. There was an institution there, in which there were a number of coloured females of abandoned character, and I acknowledge that in every place women and drink were the chief objects of my thoughts. I was still in the "gall of bitterness, and the bond of iniquity."

We left Allahabad early in the morning, because of the excessive heat, and marched away until we came to some pleasant spot where we could find water. We encamped in the heat of the day, and marched only during the early morning, and continued that practice until we came to Benares. Benares is a very large and extensive town, situated beside the Ganges, about five hundred miles from Calcutta. At the end of each day's march, the church in the regiment would look out for some favourable quiet spot where they could meet together for worship. But I still practised iniquity with my ungodly companions with greediness.

A few of us, on one occasion, got a half-gallon of a strong liquor called arrack, and drank it, forgetting that we had a hell to escape and a heaven to obtain. God was not in all our thoughts, and we lived as if we had no soul to be saved. We did not know our lost condition, and therefore did not seek salvation through the blood of the Lamb ; but we used to drown all such thoughts, and make ourselves merry in singing the song of the drunkard, offending God, destroying both body and soul, and corrupting one another. The pious soldiers, on the other hand, who "feared the Lord, spake often one to another, and the Lord hearkened and heard it, and a book of remembrance was written before him for them that feared the Lord, and that thought upon his name." O how different were the two classes ! I was breaking God's commandments—they were keeping them. I was destroying my soul, and ruining my constitution—they were seeking the salvation of their souls, and preserving their health. I was on the road to hell—they were on the way to heaven. My joys were like the crackling of thorns under a pot. They left a sting behind, and were the cause of much grief and bitter reflections ; but their "joys were unspeakable and full of glory." I was at "enmity with God,"—they were "reconciled to him through the

death of his Son." I was "without God, and
without Christ, and without hope in the world,"
— they had "Christ in their hearts, the hope
of glory." I was naked, and like the man
possessed with the "legion of devils," out of my
mind—they were "clothed and in their right
mind." O surely the way of transgressors is hard,
even in this life; and if grace does not prevent, it
will be hard throughout eternity.

From Benares, we continued marching many
days, until we came to Cawnpore, where we remained for a considerable time, receiving men of
different regiments from Madras and Bombay, to
fill up vacancies. Whilst in the hospital there, I
saw the men that were wounded at Bhurtpore.
Some had their arms cut off by the shoulder-
blade, others with their legs amputated, and some
with their bodies full of wounds and scars.
Wounds are very dangerous in a hot climate,
and have a bad smell in consequence of the heat.
I have seen it melting the marrow out of the
bones of men whose limbs had been amputated.
O the dreadful effects of war!

I was not long out of the hospital until the
Lord laid his rod upon me. I took fever and
ague, and a serjeant of the same regiment was
seized with the same troubles, and went into the
hospital along with me. We lay close beside one
another. The ague left him, but the fever continued, and he died. The Lord, however, spared
me, the worst of the two; I got well, and came
out again to begin anew my old evil habits.

Surely my sins must have been very heinous and aggravated in the sight of God! But although the Lord had shown much kindness in sparing such a vile wretch as I was, whilst others were cut off before my eyes, my heart still remained hard and insensible. O what a blind, infatuated, stupid, insensible wretch was I! No mercies— no judgments—no warnings, moved me in the least. I still went on in my mad career; and had arrived now at such a pitch, as to enter into a paction with a corporal, who was one of my chief companions in sin, that when it was his turn to call over the names of the men at night, he should omit mine. He did so, and I remained out of quarters all night, in bad company of course. I am ashamed of my wickedness now, but I gloried in it then —"God be merciful to me a sinner!"

In Cawnpore the 22d regiment was quartered in cantonments. The regiment is never quartered in barracks, but in lines—such lines consisting of ten rows of thatched huts, one being apportioned to each company. The houses were long and narrow, full of windows, on each side, with neither frame nor glass in them. But there were matted shutters which they always put on the side against which the wind blew. The other side was always open on account of the hot winds that blew in the heat of the day. There were two black men employed for each company to bring water, and, with a small vessel made for the purpose, to throw it upon the side of the house.

These men remained thus employed during the heat of the day.

There was a kind of veranda, or hollow covering overhead, extending around the cantonments. Each soldier had a bedstead for himself, and they were all arranged close together on each side; and when the water was thrown on the matted shutter outside, the wind came through quite cool. The Honourable Company was at the expense of providing every accommodation for the army during our stay here. Every soldier was paid all the arrears due to him, but these were not put to a good, but a very bad use.

After this we got orders to proceed to Muttra, to join the army there, under the command of General Lake. We marched for many days, until at last we arrived at our destination. The soldiers' wives being left behind here with the heavy baggage, we set off in pursuit of Holkar and his cavalry. We had elephants to carry our tents and tent equipage. Eight double canvas tents, and two elephants to carry them, were allotted to each company. We had camels to carry our ammunition. A great number of natives accompanied the army as cooks and water-carriers to the soldiers. We had a market all the way. The market people had buffaloes to carry their luggage, and erected their temporary shops every time we pitched our camp. Women of bad character also followed the army, carrying their tents with them all the way. How busy the devil is, and how ready to seize every opportunity of ruining precious souls ! I still ran into every excess, and was led captive by him at his will.

There were contractors also who travelled with us, that is, men who were appointed to provide food for us during the march. We had butchers to kill sheep and buffaloes, and cooks to make ready our meat ; and there were men who provided arrack, which was part of the soldier's rations. When in barracks we had only half the allowance we had in camp. At times we were much parched by the heat and want of water on the line of march. We had to endure the scorching sun, burning sands, and long tedious marches through a dreary untrodden wilderness. Sometimes we had to climb up high places, at others we had to traverse low valleys filled with jungles, through which the pioneers had to cut a road for the gun-carriages. Sometimes we were much fatigued.

The quartermaster-serjeant, and some camp colour-serjeants, went before us to choose the ground where the army was to encamp. A native, who accompanied the army all the way, went along with them, carrying a tomtom, a sort of instrument shaped like a kettle-drum, which he beat with two sticks. We could hear the sound of it long before we saw the camp-colours. I have often observed, that long before we could hear the tomtom, the men would all have become quite silent—you would not hear so much as one word. The weight of our arms, accoutrements, and ammunition, hunger and thirst, and marching over bad roads, made us dumb. But whenever we heard the sound of the tomtom, new life was put into every one of us. O what chit-chat you would hear then! And what was the subject of our conversation, and the cause of our joy! O I am near the end of my day's journey. 1 shall get rest to my weary limbs, and food to satisfy my hunger, and my dram of arrack to refresh me. The very thought of this, you would think, put fresh life into every man.

There was a man belonging to the religious society I formerly mentioned as existing in our regiment, who died about two years after we came to Burhampore. When asked by his brethren, shortly before his death, what was the state of his mind in the prospect of his soon being in eternity, he replied as follows, spiritual-ising the circumstance I have just related :—" I am greatly fatigued, and quite wearied out with sin, and this sinful world, and temptations, and trouble, and disease, and pain. But I have a good ˉhope, through grace, beyond this world. I trust I shall soon be in heaven, and I am as desirous to be there as ever I was when wearied with a long march to arrive at the camp-ground ; and it puts fresh life and joy into my soul when I think that I shall soon ' enter into that rest that remaineth for the people of God.' There, Jesus will lead me and feed me beside fountains of living waters, and God himself shall wipe away all tears from my eyes." And so the man glorified his Lord and Master at the latter end of his life and in his death. To see this Christian die, strengthened the faith of his brethren.

Now the way we went was by Delhi. We had to cross a river called the Jumna. It ran very rapidly, and had nearly carried away such of our men as were little of stature. We forded it at a shallow place where the water did not reach above our loins. We carried our arms and accoutrements upon our heads, to keep them dry, until we got over to the other side. We marched through towns and villages, which were generally surrounded with walls and gates, as the enemy went before us. We had often to get a guide when we came to a village or town. The head constable provided one that knew the way, and he was given in charge to a guard in front. If he led us right he was paid for his trouble ; but, if he deceived us, his life was forfeited.

At last we nearly overtook the enemy by means of forced marches, or by what we called stealing a march. To explain this, I may state, that after we had finished one day's march we pitched our tents for the night. However, when it grew dark, we got orders to strike them quietly, and set forward again, thus going two days' march in the twenty-four hours, and this is what is meant by stealing a march. We have encamped on the same ground at night that the enemy encamped on the night before. Although they were mounted on horseback and we on foot, we pursued them so closely, that we have found the fires they had just left still burning. We

continued the pursuit until we came to the
borders of Persia, where the climate was very
cold. The enemy was there brought to a stand,
as the Persians refused to allow them to set foot
on their territories. There was therefore nothing
left for Holkar now but to fight or surrender, as
were close at his heels. He surrendered accordingly, and gave himself up to our will, and was
carried off by us as a prisoner down the same
road we came up. I cannot tell what was done
with him after his army was disbanded. I
remember, however, that I called him a coward
for giving himself up to us after so long a pursuit
without a fight, adding, at the same time, certain
words which were anything but good ; but that
was a habit I acquired in the army. To my
shame I confess it. When Holkar gave himself
up, we were encamped by the side of a large
river, called the Hyphasis, at the time covered
over with ice. There was a large mountain on
the other side, remarkably high, and which
seemed a plain on the top. I was informed that
this mountain was on the borders of Persia, and
nearly 2000 miles from Calcutta.

On the line of march, I had a comrade that
was much given to swear and drink. We were
very attentive to one another's comfort. Sometimes it was my duty to mount guard after a
sore day's march, when the first thing he would
do would be to look after my dinner, and get it
ready, and bring it to me before he took his own.
I used to do the same thing for him ; and if we

had been drinking too much the night before, we used to make up a doze of two glasses that would cure our aching heads, and banish the strange sights that we saw, and which we used to call "the horrors." At last my comrade brought on a bloody flux by drinking to excess, and even then I gave him toddy, and he died some time after. What we call toddy in India is made from a tree which is broached at a certain time by the natives. A vessel is then fastened to the tree for receiving the juice. When it is full, it is taken down. When drunk it produces the same effect in India as strong ale does in Edinburgh. As this brings on a bowel complaint when made into toddy and drunk to excess, it certainly was a bad medicine to give to my comrade, already ill with bloody flux, and in the hospital. It was supposed, however, that if cayenne pepper was put into the liquid, it would prevent it from doing any harm, and I still remember that I did this before I gave it to my comrade, who died. We both had a hand in shortening each other's days with drinking. He died in Muttra, after we returned from our long march after Holkar. When he was dying he sent for me to the hospital where he was lying. I came accordingly, and found him in the agonies of death. Being a Roman Catholic, he asked me to read from their prayer-book for him, which I did without any hesitation. I had at that time no more serious impression on my mind about my comrade's dreadful condition, and that he

was so soon to appear before his Judge, than if
he had been a brute beast. But he had an
immortal soul, and seemingly died as he had
lived—in his sins ; and if we believe the word of
God, any man dying in that condition cannot go
where Christ is ; and if he cannot go where
Christ is, there is only one other place to which
he can go, and that is—hell. O how heinous
must my sins be in the sight of God, which have
probably been instrumental in helping to ruin
many of my ungodly companions, who died in
the same condition, without repentance toward
God and faith in our Lord Jesus Christ ! These
may now be cursing me in hell for helping to
bring them there ! They are now beyond my
reach to warn them, but I shall see them all at
the day of judgment, and they will be laying
many things to my charge. Under this conviction, it is my concern to have all my thoughts,
words, and actions, brought to remembrance, so
far as the Lord may enable me to do it, although
I am convinced that I cannot know one of a
thousand of my sins, for they are as numerous as
the sands of the sea, yet I wish to keep no secrets
between God and my own soul. I desire to say
with Job—(O that it may be with my whole
heart !) — "How many are mine iniquities and
sins ? make me to know my transgression and
my sin." David could find no peace while he
covered his sins. "When I kept silence, my
bones waxed old through my roaring all the day
long. For day and night thy hand was heavy

upon me ; my moisture was turned into the
drought of summer." " I acknowledged my
sin unto thee, and mine iniquity have I not
hid. I said I will confess my transgressions
unto the Lord, and thou forgavest the iniquity of
my sin."

I am, nevertheless, condemned for breaking even
one point of the law, as if I had broken the whole ;
for the law of God is holy and spiritual, and ex-
tends to the thoughts of the heart, as well as to
the outward conduct. I believe that, in general,
the Holy Spirit of God, when he begins the good
work of regeneration in the soul, shows us sin by
the law, and then the law condemns us, and that
the same Holy Spirit makes the " law our schoolmaster to bring us to Christ " for the pardon of
our sins. He is the end of the law for righteousness to them that believe, and if I have faith to
believe in the Son of God, it is the Spirit that
works in me the work of faith with power. The
Spirit indeed is the agent, but the gospel is the
instrument ; and while all this is true, still it is
in the use of means that we are brought to repent
and to believe the gospel. It is at the cross of
Christ, when I am led by the Spirit to bring all
my sins with me, and confess them there, that I
see the exceeding sinfulness of my sins in the
sufferings of my surety. And as my eyes behold
by faith the Lamb of God that takes away my
sin in particular, it is there (even at the cross)
that my heavy load and burden of guilt is removed, and that God is glorified in extending

pardon and peace to the chief of sinners who believe on the Son of God. In Immanuel "mercy and truth meet together, righteousness and peace have kissed each other," in the salvation of all who believe. From that time we have peace with God, through Him who has "finished the work that the Father had given him to do." Then the whole Christian life becomes a continual warfare all the way to heaven—a journey through a worse wilderness spiritually than any I have gone through literally. But the Lord will bring his people through, and they will be made more than conquerors through him that loved them." O may we all be coming up through this wilderness, leaning upon our Beloved for strength, under a conscious sense of our weakness, and he will bring us safely home at last !

In the interior of India I saw great numbers of the poor blind natives on their way to the Temple of Juggernaut. . Our men asked them where they were going, and they replied "to Juggernaut." Their cheerfulness was surprising, although they knew that they should probably be crushed to death under the car of the idol, for they think that if they die by this means they will be happy for ever. These poor creatures travel hundreds of miles to Juggernaut, with few clothes upon their body, and little provision to carry them to the end of their long and painful journey. And yet they take a pleasure in it, although it is an idol they are going to worship, and that worship, too, attended with the most horrid cruelties.

These idolaters put us, who call ourselves Christians, to shame. I saw a man, almost naked, on a long pilgrimage for the purpose of obtaining pardon for his sins. He had made a vow to hold up his hand as high as he could stretch it above his head for a long period of time, and he was not to pare his nails nor comb his hair ; and he was, moreover, to fast every day during the time the sun was up. I was quite near him, and I saw that the arm he held up was quite contracted, and wasted to skin and bone, and that he could not take it down. His nails, too, had grown so long that I thought at the time they went up into the palm of his hand.

I have also seen these people go to the temple where they worshipped their idols. The steps by which they went up were washed very clean, and they proceeded very reverently, taking off their shoes, and bowing their heads all the way as they went up, praying to their idols that had eyes, but could not see, and ears, but could not hear them, and hands, but could not save them. O that we could get the Scriptures translated into their language, and circulated among them—unfurling the banners of the cross on the banks of the Ganges, and preaching Christ and Him crucified !

You would be surprised to see how many different castes there are in Bengal. Every different caste has different idols, and each caste thinks itself right, just as the different denominations in Edinburgh do. Some worship birds, four-footed beasts and creeping things, fire and water, and

the host of heaven. I have seen a man and his
wife and family all go into the river Ganges early
in the morning before the sun arose, to have family
worship. They all went into the river up to their
loins, and took off their coppra, that is their
clothes, which consisted of a cloth about the loins
and another about their head, which they called
a turban, and they wash them in the river, which
they deem sacred or holy water. Then they are
all attention to behold the sun as soon as it rises,
and the head of the family prays to it with his
eyes wide open, gazing on the object of worship
with earnest desires for an answer to his prayers
for his wife and family. I have also gone to their
market-place in the mornings, and observed that
the first thing they do, before they work or sell,
is to pray to their gods, which are no gods. These
poor idolaters shame us, who possess the revelation
of the true God and his Son Jesus Christ, whom
he has sent!

They also sit up many nights in the year,
around a great fire, singing to their idols, beating
on their tomtoms, and playing on their musical
instruments, each trying, you would think, who
would praise his idol best. You would think, to
hear the men in Bengal sing, that you listened to
women's voices, if you did not see them. They
are of a weakly constitution, owing chiefly, I suppose, to the kind of food they eat. Most of their
castes will not permit them to eat butcher meat.
Their chief diet is therefore rice and curry, not
meat curry, but fish curry or fowl curry.

There were many of the customs of India which reminded me (even though still in the "gall of bitterness, and in the bond of iniquity") of portions of Scripture I had read when a boy at school in Edinburgh.

For example, I have seen a woman grinding at the mill in their open market-place. They have two small grinding stones. The one is fastened in the ground, and the other on the top of it, with a hole in it to let down whatever they want to grind. A handle is fastened to the upper stone, by which they turn it about. The two women sit opposite one another on their haunches, and each of them takes hold of the handle of the upper grindstone with one hand and feeds it with the other. Matt. xxiv. 41. Both men and women work, eat, and do everything seated on their haunches.

One time I passed about six women collected together; their long black hair was hanging loose down their backs, and they were all crying bitterly. I inquired the reason why they wept so. They informed me that some near relative had died, and that the weeping women had been summoned to weep over the dead. The sight made me weep also. I could not help it.

I have seen a large drove of sheep following their shepherd, who went before them. The sheep "know their shepherd," and "will not follow a stranger." This is literally true.

The different castes have rules by which they go, and if any one of their number break these rules, his caste is lost, and he is excommunicated. If the person thus cut off is sorry for his offence, and wishes to be taken back again, he must suffer some punishment before he is re-admitted.

To my own knowledge there were two backsliders restored, by suffering an iron hook to be thrust into their bodies. In the body of one of them the hook was thrust in at the lowest rib ; in the body of the other, under the shoulder-blade. There was a rope attached to each of the hooks, and afterwards fastened to a beam. The beam was balanced on a high pole thrust into its centre. They were then turned round the pole, amid the rejoicings of their caste, who stood around them, beating drums, and piping on instruments of music. This is continued for some minutes, when they are taken down, and restored to their former caste. " Their sorrows shall be multiplied that hasten after another god."

There is another practice very common in India, viz., the betrothing of children when they are young by their parents. They are not, however, permitted to live together until they come of age. There is also a caste that constantly wear a silver ring upon the hand. This ring is about the thickness of a man's little finger. They place it upon the wrist, but being large, it comes down to the thick part of the hand.

After we came back to Muttra, I still lived in the practice of every sin, and, along with my ungodly companions, profaned God's holy name and his holy Sabbaths in rioting and drunkenness.

To my shame I confess that I gloried in this line
of conduct, along with my wicked companions.
My wickedness "reached up to the heavens," and
had its "foundation as deep as hell." The number
of my sins was "as the sand of the sea."

Alas for my ungodly companions, they are
beyond the reach of mercy now, and their doom
is fixed unalterably for ever! O how glad would
they be if they had only one day in this world;
but no, "time with them is no longer!"

It is very remarkable that, notwithstanding my
sinful conduct, my true character was concealed
from my superiors. I think the hearty *rataning*
I got at first, as I mentioned in the beginning,
"smartened" me up, and made me very attentive
to my duty. I was (according to the phrase)
"pretty clean," so that I was even taken notice
of, and promoted to the rank of corporal. This
promotion was not profitable to my soul. In the
first place, it puffed me up with pride; and in the
second place, the increase of my pay enabled me
still more to gratify my evil propensities, and to
indulge my old sinful habits to a greater extent
than before.

It was the corporal's duty to take some men
with him and draw the company's provisions
every day for a week, and to serve them out to
the men. Now there are five corporals in a company, so it came to my turn to perform this duty
once every five weeks. I had to get, and serve
out to the men, meat, bread, and arrack, every
day for a week. When it came my turn to be

orderly, and when I served out the arrack, I did not give the men their full measure, because all that was over was my own. In this way I had sometimes a bottle, and at other times more or less to myself, out of what I had wronged the men by short measure. I did not think at the time, however, that the Lord was present marking down all my conduct, and that he would bring me to account for all my unjust ways, as well as for everything else.

All the time that I served in the 81st regiment, from the year 1797 until the beginning of 1803, Lieutenant-Colonel Hamilton was our commanding officer, and was with the regiment while I remained in it. When he knew that I had left his regiment (and the way he knew that was by my having on part of the uniform of the 81st, and part of the uniform of the 22d regiment), he called me, and not knowing my name, said, " My lad, did you belong to my regiment ?" I answered, " Yes, please your honour, I did." He then said he never knew there was such a man in the regiment. Officers should know the good men of their regiments, but the only men he knew were those who had been before him for crimes deserving punishment. The adjutant, whose name was Lieutenant Andrews, being with him, he asked my character. The adjutant gave me a most excellent character, and on that account the colonel seemed sorry that I had left his regiment, although I had been guilty of crimes that deserved to be punished most severely, as the reader may know by what I have already mentioned. Indeed, during the time I was in the regiment I was a hidden hypocrite.

There was a dispute before we left the Cape of Good Hope between Brevet-Colonel Brock of the 81st regiment and Captain Menzies of the 22d regiment, grenadier company, and it was decided by a duel, in which Captain Menzies shot Colonel Brock. It is worthy of note that, although man winked at this crime, yet Captain Menzies, two years afterwards, was himself killed at Bhurtpore. I am not saying that this was a judgment from the hand of the Lord, but it is certain that the Lord does not approve of fighting duels.

The commanding officer of the 22d regiment was Lieutenant-Colonel Mercer, who continued with the regiment until we came down to Muttra, where he left us. We there received another commanding officer—the strictest I ever knew. When he entered on the command, he commenced to drill us as if we had been recruits, and carried us through all the different degrees of discipline until he had the regiment able to go through the manual and platoon exercise like clock-work. If men were found drunk on parade, he inflicted a fortnight's confinement, and fed them on boiled rice, as a punishment for the first offence. For the second offence he inflicted two hundred lashes on the bare back. It was under this officer I was made a corporal. It was said that he was a great gambler, and that he gambled away the pay of the regiment. Whether this were true or

not, we certainly got no pay for about six
months, although we always had our rations.  In
consequence of this, all the private soldiers agreed
(non-commissioned officers excepted), that on a
particular morning when on parade, they should
not obey the command from the commanding
officer, but would proceed in regular marching
order to the residence of General Dickens, who
lived about a mile distant, to lodge a complaint
against the colonel.  Accordingly, when the day
appointed arrived, they made arrangements to
carry their design into execution.  It happened
that our colonel was unwell, and that being the
case, the officer next in seniority took the command.    That officer chanced to be a captain.
When the regiment was assembled, the men in
companies, headed by their respective officers,
proceeded to the parade-ground, and formed into
open column, the officers at the same time taking
their usual places.  The commanding officer now
came forward, took his station in front, and
gave the word of command.  Not a man, however, obeyed, except the officers and non-commissioned officers.

It happened that day to be my turn to be corporal of the quarter-guard.  This being the conduct of the regiment, the commanding officer
ordered every tenth man to be confined in the
guard-house, and I being on the same guard, had
to plant sentinels over them.  After these men
had been confined, all the privates in the regiment first fixed bayonets, secondly shouldered

arms, and then marched off—the band playing and the drums beating alternately, all the way to the residence of General Dickens. When they arrived at the General's, they halted, and formed in line in front of the house in the most orderly manner. A man from each of the ten companies now stepped out in front, and proceeded with his comrades to the General's, to lodge a complaint, in writing, I believe, against the Colonel. After the complaint had been given in, they marched regularly back again, with music and drums, and then dismissed. After dismissing, the first thing they did was to come to the guard-house, and release all the prisoners. I believe if I or any of the guard had resisted, or tried in any way to prevent them, they would have run us through. When we saw, therefore, that the whole regiment was of the same mind, we just let them have their own will. I was in the midst of the prisoners when the mutineers rushed in and took them out. They offered no violence either to me or any of the guard.

Shortly after this, we saw an army of infantry and cavalry, composed of black soldiers, with field pieces in front, and General Dickens commanding them, marching towards us. On this the guard turned out, and formed in line to salute the General, and all the regiment ran and formed in a line in front of the guard. General Dickens then formed his black army in line of battle, artillery and cavalry in front. After the two lines were formed, facing each other, the General moved

out on horseback and says, "Twenty-second, take
the command from me." (If I remember right,
they had their bayonets fixed, and their arms
shouldered). "Rear rank, take double open
order—march." They did so. "Order arms."
Next—"handle arms"—and last, and most dis-
graceful to them—"Ground arms." Saying this
he gave command to his black cavalry to charge
upon the 22d regiment, and drive them from their
arms. He then made them strip off their
accoutrements and lay them on the ground by
companies, and ordered off the men to their
cantonments, without arms and accoutrements, to
do no duty.

Next, the guard was relieved by sepoys, that is,
black native soldiers. I, being then the corporal
of the quarter-guard in Muttra, delivered up the
two stands of colours belonging to the 22d regiment, along with the rest of the guard, and had,
to my great grief, to ground my arms and take
off my accoutrements, and share the fate of my
companions.

This incident appeared to me afterwards, a
wonderful illustration of the manner in which the
Lord Jesus Christ comes to sinners in the preaching of the gospel. The General came to the rebellious band, ordering them to lay down their
arms. The men heard and obeyed the command;
they laid down their arms and submitted to his
will, although aware that they should be visited
with punishment. In like manner the Lord
Jesus Christ comes to sinners by the preaching

of his word. He finds them in a state of rebellion, and he conquers them by the power of his word and the influence of his Spirit, and lays them low. He likewise employs afflictive dispensations, and even their very sins, for the purpose of humbling them before him, and of bringing them to their " right mind."

Our Lieutenant-Colonel continued in bad health until he died. I heard that on the very day on which he breathed his last, which was at some distance from the regiment, he ordered one of his black servants to be flogged in his presence. After he died, I was informed that there were none but his servants to bury him, and that they buried him as if he had been a dog. A short time after this, we got orders to leave Muttra, and to embark in boats prepared to receive us. We had, however, to march a few days before we came to them. The place to which we were ordered was Burhampore.

One day I felt inclined to read my Bible, and I went to a quiet place under the shadow of some trees, and lay down upon the green grass. As I was reading some portion of the word of God, I experienced a delight to which I had long been a stranger; but I knew nothing of myself as a sinner, or of Christ as a Saviour. Whilst I was thus employed one of the soldiers found me out, and informed me that there was a letter for me. This letter turned out to be from my parents, and I wondered at it at the time, as I had not got one from them for years; but I soon forgot it, and returned to my old practices, and continued in them all the time we remained in Muttra.

At length, I think about the end of 1806, we set out for Burhampore, but without arms. It requires a great number of boats to hold a regiment of soldiers. I think there were about twenty men in each boat. These boats resemble wooden houses; they are roofed over to screen the passengers from the scorching heat of the sun. Each boat is manned by black men. We used to sail all day, and rest all night. I think we sailed about seven hundred miles down the river, until we came to Burhampore. Every morning before we loosened from the banks of the river to sail down with the stream, the native boatmen would lave the bows of the boat with water, and pray to their idols. They scarcely do anything without praying first. They are far more zealous in serving their idols than we are in serving the living and true God. A more pleasant sail than that down that river I think I never had in my life. It is indeed a beautiful part of the world, and presented a pleasing sight. The sun shining gloriously, the birds singing, the fields filled with fruit-trees laden with fruit, and with indigo and cotton, and almost every other thing for the comfort and good of man and beast. Likewise we could see rivers running in every direction to water the ground. Had the Psalmist been there, he would have said, "How marvellous are thy works, Lord God Almighty!"

But I was blind, stupid, and ignorant. I never saw God in his works, and his goodness in forming them for sinful man. I believe I have done the heathen great injury by my conduct, which I have no doubt prevented some of them from receiving the gospel. In coming down the river I coveted something, and bought it from the natives ; but, to my shame I acknowledge it, I would not give what they required for it, and took it away from them, and gloried in the fact with my ungodly companions. I observed in sailing down a great many fires on the banks of the river. These were kindled by the natives, who do not bury their dead like us, but burn them by the side of the river ; and it is the request of many before they die to be carried down to the river side to breathe their last. There they will lay them down, and see their friends piling up the wood that is to burn their bodies to ashes.

In sailing down the Ganges, one of our boats sprung a leak, and was in great danger of going down in a deep place, far from the shore. But a kind Providence had so ordered it, that another boat came alongside and saved the crew. The passengers had just time to step out of the one boat into the other, when she went down. They were unable to save or bring away with them anything but what they had on them, so far as I can recollect.

There was a man and his wife, with whom I was intimately acquainted, who were in the boat that foundered, and they told me that they had just time to bring what little money they had before the boat went down, and they very narrowly escaped from going down with it. One of the soldiers, however, who could swim and dive, and who had his money with him in the boat when she sunk, grieved to lose his all. He ventured to dive down to recover what he had lost; but it cost him his life, for he never came up again. Notwithstanding all these remarkable providences and signal interpositions on our behalf, none of us seemed inclined to lay our preservation to heart. The more hardened and depraved amongst us ascribed our deliverance to chance, and to our own activity and exertions. So we went on frowardly in the error of our ways, repaying the goodness and long-suffering of the Lord with ingratitude—and our foolishness was not hid from him.

At length we arrived at Burhampore, where we were stationed for about the space of three years. Burhampore is nearly one hundred miles from Calcutta, with large and commodious barracks near the river side. After we landed, we got our arms and accoutrements back again; the outbreak at Muttra and the cause of it was strictly looked into, and the conduct of the colonel in making a bad use of the regimental funds, and in neglecting to pay the men their money when it became due, was disapproved of. As the colonel was dead, and of course could not defend himself, all the blame was laid to his charge, and so the matter ended.

I now come back to myself, and confess I am ashamed to. do so. I was outwardly moral and decent at home, but at heart I was depraved. Still I was restrained from gross outward immorality on account of the causes I mentioned before. But when I entered the army the inward depravity of my heart gradually broke out. I was bad in Guernsey, I was worse at the Cape of Good Hope, and still worse after landing in India ; but I was exceedingly sinful, and polluted, and polluting, for the first twelve months after I came to Burhampore. I used to be very agreeable formerly when drinking along with my ungodly companions, and they loved my company, but here I became rough and quarrelsome. I used formerly to remember what I said when under the influence of drink, but now I sometimes lost all recollection of what I said or did. Many a time have I made myself worse than a beast with it. I remember one time in particular, I drank to such excess as to be unable to walk or stand, and was obliged to lie down on the ground and wallow in my own filthiness, like a sow wallowing in the mire. Some of my companions, pitying my condition, lifted me up and threw me into the river, knowing I could swim, and my heart warmed with gratitude and love to them for so doing.

There was a Scotchman I fell in with at Burhampore belonging to another regiment, and as I was always particularly fond of my countrymen in foreign lands, I got him and a few more to sit up all night to converse about Scotland over half a gallon of arrack, and we got quite the worse of drink. So you see I did not only do evil to myself, but I was the cause of others doing evil; I did not only corrupt myself, but became a corrupter of others.

I remember one occasion on which one of my most intimate companions and I got up in the morning, and went to the place where the arrack was sold, and there, before stopping, drank nine glasses a piece. I had to mount guard soon after. The sergeant-major inspected the guard, but did not observe me the worse of drink, at least that I knew of; and I, being corporal of the guard, had to go to the front as fugleman. However, after I mounted guard, I lay down on the guard-bed, and fell into a sleep like a dead man. Some time in the afternoon I awoke, and found myself in the barrack-room, lying in my own bed, with all my accoutrements off me, and a comrade corporal standing by my bedside. "Are not you a pretty fellow to be on guard, and you dead drunk?" That corporal seeing my condition in the guard-room, had taken my duty, and I was to do the same by him when it came to be *his* turn. Many a one has been broke and flogged for the crime of which I had just been guilty.

I well recollect the first man who died after we came to India. He was a Scotchman, and he died drunk. After drinking to excess, he fell asleep with the stock about his neck, and in the

morning he was found quite dead and black in
the face. Now this was a dreadful condition to
leave the world in, and appear before a holy God.
We can have no hope of that man hereafter,
if we believe the Word of God. All this
then I knew, and yet took no warning, for I
have often been in the same condition, and a
kind providence spared me. And why *me*, I
cannot tell. The Lord only knows. One morning I got orders to take a party of men with me
and go to the magazine to get ammunition for the
company to shoot with, to which I belonged. As
usual, I went first to the canteen to get my morning dram. On the way I lighted a cigar, and put
it into my mouth, and went into the middle of
the magazine, smoking all the way, heedlessly
and imprudently. I did not bethink me of what
I was doing, until the quarter-master sergeant,
who was there to serve out the ammunition, cried
out in surprise and terror, " Corporal Flockhart,
what do you mean ? Do you intend to blow up
the magazine ?" If I remember right, these were
his words. Surprised and confounded, I quickly
took the cigar out of my mouth, and put it under
my foot. Now there might have been loose
powder scattered over the floor, as there often
happens to be, when serving out cartridges ; and
if there had, the whole magazine would have
been blown up in a moment, and we all should
have been hurried into eternity. I took no time
to think what I was about, or what I ought to
have done under the circumstances ; but, instead

of putting the burning end into my mouth, put it under my foot. The Lord, however, was pleased to preserve me, notwithstanding my repeated provocations. Truly a kind providence has followed me all my days. Well may I wonder at it, and say, "Why me, blessed Lord, who so repeatedly and heedlessly was rushing along the downward road to destruction?"

The quarter-master sergeant did not report me; if he did, I never heard any more about it, and while I remained in a state of nature, I thought no more about it. O how blind and ungrateful is man, while in a natural state, to his ever-kind and unwearied Protector and Preserver, from dangers by night and by day! He neither sees nor acknowledges the hand of the Lord in preserving or delivering him, but ascribes all to chance, and his own energy and activity.

> "I see a bush that burns with fire,
> Unconsumed amid the flame!
> Turn aside the sight t'admire,
> I, the living wonder am.
> Tell it unto sinners, tell
> I am—I am out of hell!
>
> "I see a stone that hangs on air!
> I see a spark in ocean live!
> Kept alive with death so near,
> I to God the glory give.
> Ever tell—to sinners tell,
> I am—I am out of hell!"

Truly the long-suffering of God in Christ Jesus to me, in particular, is very great.

## PART II.—HIS CONVERSION

How mysterious the means used by the Lord to bring sinners from their evil ways! This was strikingly manifested in my case, as will appear from what I am going to relate. One day I had been the worse of drink, and, as was my custom, lay down on my bed to sleep off its effects. I was in this condition when the orderly-serjeant of the company awoke me, to go and show the officer regimental orders. I told him I was not orderly. He insisted, however, that I should go and do what he desired me immediately. I said I would do no such thing. He then told me, if I did not do as he desired, he would put me in the guard-house. I replied, if you do, I will report you to the officer. I went accordingly ; but while on the way, he sent an active serjeant after me to detain me until he got a corporal and file of the guard to apprehend me, which they did, and brought me a prisoner to the guard-house. This was the first step God, in his mysterious providence, employed to apprehend me in my mad career. It certainly was my duty to obey the serjeant's orders ; but being the worse of drink, and suddenly awakened out of my sleep, I refused. In consequence of this, I was ordered to be tried by a court-martial for disobedience and insolence to my superior officer. This was the first time I was in prison, and I remained in it three days. During this period, I employed myself, along with the other prisoners, in trying myself by the articles of war.

I had serious thoughts about the result, and really expected to be flogged. In due time my case came on. I was tried, and sentenced to be reduced from a corporal to a private, and to receive one hundred and fifty lashes. Lieutenant-Colonel Dalrymple, who commanded the regiment, remitted the corporal punishment. Drum-major M'Kee cut the stripes off my arm before all the regiment. I was glad, no doubt, to escape the flogging, but reducing me to the rank of private humbled my proud spirit. I took it very sore to heart, but it produced no sanctifying effect on me at the time, and I still went on in my old ways. A number of my old companions and I met in the barracks. It seems I was foremost in wickedness, as I employed my time in speaking abominable language till they were all like to fall down with laughing. It is a most mysterious circumstance that I should be drawn out from the entire company, while the bent of my heart was to commit sin.

In India it is no uncommon thing for streams of fire to descend from the clouds, owing, I suppose, to the great heat. On one occasion I saw a stream of fire in the form of a sword, and soon after, the Lord laid his rod upon me for my sins. I fell sick, reported myself, and was sent to the hospital. This was the second step the Lord took to bring me to my right mind. As I had none of my former companions to keep the time from hanging heavy on my hands, I had recourse to reading, and finding Cook's Voyages, I perused it with much relish. This gave me a taste for reading; I thirsted for more, and Providence cast "Alleine's Alarm" in my way. In reading that portion of it which speaks of the Day of Judgment, and of the whole human race appearing before the Lord Jesus Christ, I felt an unusually solemn impression on my mind. I was convinced of the truth of what I had read, and felt assured that I too would be there, and would have an awful account to give in. After reading the book I laid it down.

In speaking to the patients in the hospital, I used to swear whenever I spoke. The Lord is not at a loss for instruments to accomplish his purposes. He employed an Irish lad to reprove me. On one occasion when I was blaspheming, he said to me, "What a swearer you are!" I replied, "Did I swear?" "Yes, you did," was the answer. Well, I thought with myself, if I swear, and do not know when I do so, it is certainly high time to give up the practice, and especially when such as you reprove me. Henceforth I was upon my guard when I spoke, lest an oath should involuntarily escape my lips. Conscience flew in my face and made me so afraid, that for a fortnight I was engaged in learning to speak fluently without swearing. I was thus enabled to break off swearing, and determined not to do so any more.

The next step I took was to forsake the company of those that swore. There were six of us in a mess, and we were all swearers. I said, "Cut off my mess, I shall eat by myself." They asked me the reason I would not eat with them. I replied, "Because you swear." This being done, I retired to a table by myself, and asked God's blessing on my food, in the name of the Lord Jesus Christ, and got an answer to my prayer. I think I shall never forget how sweet that meal was to me. It had a different relish from what it had before. The reader will see how gradually the Lord drew me with the cords of love and with the bands of a man.

Knowing that the serjeant of the hospital was a religious man, I asked him for the loan of a religious book, which he gave me. It was his duty to allow any of the patients, who were able, and felt inclined, to take a walk on the flat roof of the hospital after the sun went down. I may mention that there was a battlement all round the roof of the hospital to keep people from falling over. Now, my mind being seriously impressed, I had no pleasure in talking with worldly people. I therefore forsook their company, and joined the pious serjeant. Seeing that I was very desirous to read religious books, he told me that reading too many would tend to confuse my mind, and advised me to study the Bible. I took his advice, and forsook the company of my worldly companions, (which caused them to reproach me). Their reproaches, however, did not tend to discourage me. They tended rather to make me more decided in joining the serjeant, and casting in my lot with the people of God.

The serjeant had a private room for himself, and he told me that there was a person who came and united with him in family worship, and if I chose to join them, he would make me welcome. I was very glad of the offer, and went regularly, and the Lord blessed the means of grace to my soul. Sometimes the serjeant read a sermon of Flavel's, or spoke from the Word of God, and my mind would be deeply impressed with the belief that he knew everything that I did. At another time the thought came into my mind that the Lord was whispering into his ear everything about me. I can see now that it was the Spirit of Christ telling me everything I did, as in the case of the woman. I was gradually melted down. I said to him that I would like to be a Christian. He said that the life of the Christian was a continual warfare. I replied that, warfare or no warfare, I was willing to engage in it. What the serjeant said to me in 1807 has been fully verified in my experience ever since, and will be till I give up the ghost.

I began now to go to an empty ward to confess my sins alone before God, and to review my past life. At such times, when the patients saw me, they all burst into such fits of laughter as almost cracked their jaws. I knew the patients that laughed at me, and remarked that not one of them came out of the hospital alive.

I still attended the meetings held by the serjeant, and at times my heart would be so overcome with the love of Christ that I would return home quite happy. I thought all the angels of God surrounded me rejoicing (see Luke xv.), and that the Spirit was applying the blood of Christ to wash away my sins, putting these sins at the same time upon my head, and I felt such a weight upon me that I was hardly able to look up. Even in this state I would have been glad to depart, but "God's thoughts are not as our thoughts, nor his ways as our ways." The Lord ordered it otherwise. I fell asleep, and when I awoke a dark horror was upon my mind ; "the sorrows of death compassed me, the pains of hell gat hold upon me ; I found trouble and sorrow." The messenger of Satan was sent to buffet me. I was led into the "wilderness to be tempted of the devil." Awful thoughts came into my mind. I thought I had committed the unpardonable sin, and had sold my birthright. Conscience awoke, and set my past sins in order before me. God seemed to frown upon me. I did not know what to say or do. All hope of being saved was gone. The tempter said to me that all I had experienced was only a delusion. He even tempted me to take away my own life. When walking on the top of the hospital, he tempted me to throw myself over the battlements, and I really thought I should have been overcome. However, he was thwarted in that, as I did not go there again. There was a well at the back of the hospital, and he urged me strongly to throw myself into it. I said to the serjeant of the hospital, "Tie me to the bed at night, and keep me sure, in case he should overcome me." The serjeant could not enter into the nature of my temptations, and of course did not do as I desired him. I cannot enter into a detail of all the temptations I was subjected to; the two I have mentioned will serve as specimens. I consider the language of the apostle, in Romans vii. 9, not inapplicable to my situation at that time, "but when the commandment came, sin revived, and I died." Sin, that had been asleep before, came like a giant upon me. I saw myself in the mirror of God's law. That law was spiritual, and extended to the thoughts and intents of my heart. Dreadful and blasphemous thoughts, like sparks out of a chimney, now came out of my heart. I was afraid to open my Bible, or even to look up, for fear the Lord would send a thunderbolt out of Heaven to crush me. I heard, as it were, a voice from Heaven, saying, "Confess your sins, confess your sins." This went like a dagger to my heart, and I could get no rest. For nearly a month I could get no sleep. I was afraid, if I fell asleep, I should open my eyes in hell. This had the effect of making me look over my past life, and to call to remembrance my past sins, what I had done, where I had been, what company I had kept, and what sins I had been guilty of.

After my sins had been thus set before me, the Lord scourged me for them, and made them bitter to me. I was led by the Spirit, with a broken spirit and a bleeding soul, to the "fountain opened," pleading for mercy, through the blood of the Lamb, to get my wounded spirit healed, my troubled conscience calmed, and my burdened soul freed from its load of guilt. Thus I continued for months. I took my Bible, and went to the most sequestered spot I could find. Being ignorant of the Bible, and my mind in darkness, I did not know where I should begin, or what part of the Word of God I should first read. I cannot describe the distressed state of my mind. I was in the horrible pit of nature, and in the miry clay of original and actual sin. As I was a patient in the hospital, I could spend two or three hours a day in private by myself, and not be missed. I used to spend whole nights in reading and meditation, and in confessing my sins.

Thus I continued persevering in the use of every means. I never ceased to pray night and day. Satan would often suggest to my mind that I would be in hell at night. I resisted him again in that temptation. I knew that he was telling lies. I found out that the Lord would not tell the devil that I would be there at twelve o'clock at night. Another temptation of his was this. I was in the serjeant's mess. He (the serjeant) kept a luxurious table, and the devil persuaded me to leave off eating with him, under the pretence that I was pampering the flesh. I therefore left the serjeant to eat by myself. I chose for my dinner what they call curry (or boiled rice), and brought down my body to a perfect skeleton. Satan, moreover, put me into such a slavish fear, that I was afraid to tell anybody, until at last I became so weak that I had to tell. I told another serjeant that the meat was cursed, and that I was afraid to eat. I found out, soon after this, that " every creature of God is good, and nothing to be refused if it be received with thanksgiving ; for it is sanctified by the Word of God and prayer."

While I was at dinner, my mind was so much on the rack, that I placed the Bible on the table, and put my finger on the passage, reading a word or two of the above-mentioned verses—then I would take a bite or two, and so on, till I had finished my meal. In this way I resisted the devil until he fled from me, and I gradually recovered my health.

A church had been formed in the regiment some time previously, and a few of the members used to come to the serjeant's room. There they were informed of the state of my mind, and of the temptations to which I had of late been subjected, and, gathering around me, told me to " believe on the Lord Jesus Christ and I should be saved." I tried all I could, but believe I could not. It was as impossible for me to believe at that time, as it would have been for me to lift Edinburgh Castle and cast it into the sea. I required to be convinced of the sin of unbelief. " And when he is come, he will reprove the world

of sin, and of righteousness, and of judgment :
of sin, because they believe not on me." What
they said to me made me worse, if worse could be.
While I remained in a state of unbelief, I seemed
to be tried in the balances of the sanctuary, and
found wanting. I had no faith. I was like a
man in hell. While in this condition I went away
to my own ward, and cried for mercy through the
blood of the Lamb. I spent the whole night in
this way.

I still persevered in reading the Bible, in confessing my sins, and in praying to God. I was
like Noah's dove, I could "find no rest for the sole
of my foot." Or like the man-slayer fleeing to
the "city of refuge," with the "avenger of blood"
at his heels. Or, like Lot among the Sodomites,
when he went out to persuade his sons-in-law to
flee from the guilty city ; or rather, when he went
out to expostulate with his abandoned and accursed
fellow-citizens when they had encompassed his
dwelling, I was surrounded with the blackguards
of hell, when the "Lord put forth his hand, and
pulled me in." On one occasion the serjeant came
to me at a critical moment, and asked me to ac-
company him to a quiet place to sing a hymn, and
to engage in prayer. We sung the fourth and
fifth verses of the 32d Psalm of Watt's collec-
tion ;—

> "Whilst I my inward guilt suppress'd,
>     No quiet could I find ;
> Thy wrath lay burning in my breast,
>     And rack'd my tortured mind.

Then I confess'd my troubled thoughts,
　My secret sins reveal'd;
Thy pard'ning grace forgave my faults,
　Thy grace my pardon seal'd."

Whilst singing the last verse, I said in my heart,
"I have done all this—I have confessed my sins;"
then a thought came into my mind, quick as lightning—I must let all my doings fall to the ground.
When I was enabled to do that, I felt that I
deserved nothing but hell, and fully expected that
it would be my portion. Then the Lord, the
Spirit, stretched out his hand and brought me in
by Christ the door. Of his own sovereign pleasure
he did this. I was expecting hell, and he gave me
a heaven in my soul. Surprising mercy! What
a translation from darkness to light, from the
kingdom of darkness to the kingdom of God's
dear Son! My guilt removed and my pardon
sealed, peace flowed like a river into my soul.
"Therefore, being justified by faith, we have
peace with God through our Lord Jesus Christ."
My "faith came from hearing, and hearing by
the word of God." It did not come from man,
nor from myself, but from God. It was God's
gift, and Christ was the author of it. This
blessed truth suggests to my mind that passage
in Corinthians—"For God, who commanded the
light to shine out of the darkness, hath shined in
our hearts, to give the light of the knowledge of
the glory of God in the face of Jesus Christ."
And this was fulfilled in my experience at that
time. I felt that light, and that life, and that
joy, coming into my heart; not into my head,

but into my heart.  My heart was warmed with his "love shed abroad in it by the Holy Ghost given unto me," and I rejoiced with "joy unspeakable and full of glory."  I now saw the Bible to be a new book, and was able, in some measure, to enter into the spirit of the apostle, where he says—"And hath given us an understanding, that we may know him that is true, and we are in him that is true, even in his Son Jesus Christ.  This is the true God and eternal life."

I now began to see that all my trials and afflictions for the last two years had been designed for my everlasting good.  All this time, indeed, my mind was on the rack.  My spirit was wounded, and a "wounded spirit who can bear?"  That wounded spirit the Lord healed by the application of the blood and righteousness of his dear Son.  I had seen a book somewhere in which the people of God are represented as entering into a covenant with the Lord.  I therefore resolved to go to a secret place, and read such passages as the following :— "They shall ask the way to Zion, with their faces thitherward, saying, Come, and let us join ourselves to the Lord in a perpetual covenant that shall not be forgotten."—"Gather my saints together unto me; those that have made a covenant with me by sacrifice."—"Also the sons of the stranger, that join themselves to the Lord, to serve him, and to love the name of the Lord, to be his servants, every one that keepeth the

Sabbath from polluting it, and taketh hold of my covenant." I began to reason thus with myself before the Lord. I am now twenty-nine years of age—what an old sinner I am! I have served the devil all my life, and done no good. Wherever I have been, I have done evil. And who knows the amount of evil? Who knows what evil I have done, not only to my own soul, but to the souls of men, women, and children who may now be cursing me in hell, as the author of their misery? I experienced the most bitter remorse, when I reflected that these persons were now beyond my reach, and their doom fixed unchangeably for ever.

There was one man in particular, a companion of mine in sin, whose unhappy fate occasioned me deep distress. Although he died in the hospital, I dared not to visit him on his death-bed, lest the Lord, in his righteous indignation, should "take me away with a stroke." My constant prayer at this time was, "Oh, Lord, if it be thy pleasure, spare me as long in thy service as I have been in Satan's, and make me as zealous in saving souls, and in converting sinners by my good example, as I once was in destroying souls, and ruining my fellow-men by my bad example. I know that I can never make amends unto thee for the evil I have done; but I wish to show my displeasure against my former ways, when I lived in ignorance and unbelief. Here I am, willing to be employed as thy servant in any capacity, whatever be the result. Whether it be freedom or a prison, sickness or health, life or death—here I am, do with me what thou wilt."

Here I signed my name to the covenant I had made with God and myself; and I believe that through the grace of God, I have been enabled to perform my vows, though imperfectly, from that hour till the present time, the 4th day of February 1855. I appeal to all those who have known me in Edinburgh or elsewhere. I think the Lord has answered the first petition. He has even spared me longer to serve him than I served the devil. I cannot, however, say that I have served the Lord without sin. I hope the Lord will forgive the sin of my most holy things. I desire to cast myself and my duties at the foot of the cross, and take Christ and his merits, and satisfaction, and rest upon him alone, and to acknowledge myself an eternal debtor to sovereign grace and redeeming love.

With regard to the *second* petition (or second part of my prayer), I cannot, of course, be expected to speak with decision on this side of the grave. The day of judgment alone can reveal to what extent it has been heard and answered.

In the hospital, I began to read the Bible to the patients, and to pray with them. The first person I tried to do good to had been an old companion of mine in sin. I thought I should be able to convert him. I was, however, disappointed. Like Melancthon, I found that old Adam was too strong for young Robert. The result of this attempt grieved my heart. I tried another. He

had once been a professor in the church in the
22d regiment. He had a great deal of head
knowledge of the Scriptures, and was very
zealous for a while, but in "time of temptation
fell away." He yielded to the sin of uncleanness,
and became worse at last than any I saw in the
regiment. The Chaplain came to see him, and
reproved him for reading a certain book, telling
him at the same time that he should read the
Bible. This he objected to do, but upon grounds
I do not remember. He afterwards told me his
temptation, and described to me how he had fallen.
While he was in the hospital his entire body became swollen, and his appetite increased to a
frightful degree. In this condition I visited him
to read the Bible to him, but he refused to hear
me. Soon after he died. The fate of this man
served as a beacon to me. It showed me how far
a man may proceed in a profession of religion, and
yet after all turn out to be a hypocrite at last.
The judgment-like death of this man made a
great impression on me.

There was another individual, also a professor
of religion, who came in like manner to an unhappy end. He and I used to attend a prayer
meeting together, early in the morning, while it
was yet dark. He knew that I was under strong
convictions on account of sin, and that I was seeking the Lord. I remember one morning, after the
prayer meeting was over, he said to me, "Well,
Robert, have you found peace yet?" I replied,
"No; I have not." On which he directed me to

the second chapter of the Epistle of the Ephesians, saying, "That chapter will tell you what you are by nature, and what you must be by grace." Well, to my astonishment, this man got intoxicated by drink, and his conscience lashed him when he became sober. To drown its reproaches he got drunk a second time, and this, of course, made matters worse, by adding fuel to fire. In this awful state of mind he went to his knapsack and got a razor, and cut his throat from ear to ear. I was the first who saw him after the dreadful deed. I found him lying in a shed at the back of the barracks at Burhampore, where a horse used to be sheltered during the heat of the day. This was another awful warning to me to avoid the sins by which these men had been destroyed.

I remember at another time going to hear a sermon preached by a soldier, and was particularly struck by one of his remarks. He said that the object of every one who came to hear the gospel should be to meet with Christ. He said, moreover, that they who did not find him would go away mourning as a dove mourns during the absence of her mate. At that time, when the sermon was done, I went near to the place where the unhappy man destroyed himself, and sat down upon a bank, my heart almost broken, and my mind dark. I said, "Blessed Lord, I went to seek thee, and did not find thee;" and then, mentioning the words of the soldier, "I go mourning as a dove during the absence of her mate." I did not continue long in this state of mind till I got an answer to my prayer, and experienced a gracious sense of the Lord's presence. Truly the Lord "moves in a mysterious way" to perform his wonderful works among the children of men !

I may remark that whenever I found any happiness or delight in devoting myself to his service, the devil was exceedingly busy in trying to deprive me of my comfort, throwing his fiery darts at me, tossing me up and down, and endeavouring to persuade me that my religious convictions and impressions were all a delusion. Instead of being discouraged by these temptations, I was only led to repair more frequently to a throne of grace. I was beginning to understand his devices, and also to know something of the word of God. His temptations made me search the Scriptures, so that by and by I got better acquainted with them.

About this time I was informed that a missionary was to preach a sermon at a little distance from the hospital. As I was earnestly engaged in seeking after Christ, I scaled the wall surrounding the hospital, in the hospital dress, and went to hear the sermon. I sat down in a place where I thought nobody would see me, and listened attentively till the service was done. As soon as the meeting was over, I came back to the hospital again, thinking I was undiscovered. Some one, however, had observed me at the meeting, and told the Missionary, who proved to be Mr. Chamberlain, a Baptist minister, and fellow-labourer of Mr. Carey's, afterwards so celebrated for his trans-

lations of the Scriptures.   Mr. Chamberlain was
kind enough to visit me, and ever after took a
deep interest in my welfare.   He instructed me
more fully in the great truths of religion, and came
frequently to the hospital to see me. · He gave me
a kind invitation to visit him and his wife, and to
join with them in family worship.   Having
mentioned Mr. Chamberlain's invitation to the
doctors, I obtained permission to go.   I likewise
requested a *doolie* to convey me to Mr Chamberlain's house, and got it, as I was still very weak.
I may here observe, for the information of the
reader, that a *doolie* resembles a bedstead with
curtains round it, and is carried on the shoulders
of four natives, two in front and two in the rear.
Well, by this conveyance I was brought to the
house of Mr Chamberlain, which was only a short
distance from the Ganges.   As riding in a doolie
was good for the health of my body, so going to
Mr Chamberlain's was good for the health of my
soul.

Mr Chamberlain had a godly wife for his help-
mate ; they were a loving couple, and equally
yoked together.   He would say, when about to
engage in family worship, "My dear, you will
raise the tune."   Mr and Mrs Chamberlain were
truly consistent Christians.   Their religion was
embodied in every action of their lives.   They
were living epistles which might be known and
read of all men.   Mr Chamberlain used to go out
in the morning, before the sun was up, to the
banks of the Ganges, to preach to the natives.

His first object was to collect a congregation. He would study to lay hold of a Brahmin, and when he got him, he would enter into conversation with him about the folly of idol-worship, and the duty and reasonableness of worshipping the true God, that made the world and all things therein, and of trusting for salvation in the Lord Jesus Christ, who came into the world to save sinners. As many came forward to hear him arguing with and refuting the Brahmins, of course a congregation was soon collected, to whom he had thus an opportunity of preaching the gospel. In this way many were turned from the service of their idols to serve the living and true God.

One morning he came home rather late, when I happened to be in his house. As soon as he came in he threw himself down on a sofa, and cried out, " My head, my head!" His wife came to him instantly to offer her assistance, saying, " My dear, why did you stay out so long to be scorched with the sun?" He replied, " When I was about to conclude my discourse, some fresh hearers came up, and I was loth to lose the opportunity." This was a lesson to me, and I never forgot it. Mr Chamberlain possessed a true missionary spirit. He infected me, and I have since endeavoured, through God's grace, to infect others. I got a slip from this geranium, and many a one, through God's blessing, I trust, has since got a slip from me.

I remained full two years in the hospital, and all that time I was under deep convictions ; being a rough stone, I got rough polishing. The Lord made my sinful life and my sinful actions as bitter as gall and wormwood. It was the inward work of the spirit that broke my hard heart and my flinty soul. He brought me through the fiery furnace of affliction, and I bless him for it. My trials and sufferings, it is true, did not feel joyous but grievous at the time ; nevertheless, afterwards they yielded unto me the peaceable fruits of righteousness. I now see the fruits, and experience the benefits of sanctified affliction, and may say with David—" It is good for me that I have been afflicted."

The Lord has many ways of bringing sinners to himself. Thus he says, by his servant Jude, " And of some have compassion, making a difference : and others save with fear, pulling them out of the fire, hating even the garment spotted with the flesh." The latter was my case. Long affliction for sin is not easily forgotten. I will never forget, all my life, how I was dealt with for my sins. That put me in remembrance of what I saw at home. When I was a boy my father had a favourite linnet, for which he had a great regard, and on which he set a high value. There happened to be a cat in the house, which, judging from her looks, seemed set on taking the linnet. My father saw what was going on, so he seized the cat, and rubbed her nose against the wires of the cage until it bled. This proved an effectual cure for the cat. And just so in my case. The punishment I underwent, and the sufferings I endured for my sins, made them so bitter and grievous to me, as led me to hate and avoid them ever after. "Before I was afflicted I went astray, but since I have been afflicted, I have kept thy word."

After my two years of affliction in the hospital, it pleased God that I got well again, and I went back to the regiment to do duty. Soon after my return, we were ordered to Calcutta, which is about seventy miles distant from Burhampore. When we reached Calcutta, we encamped in the glacis in front of Fort William, the barracks being filled with troops.

We remained here some time, and there being a church in the regiment (it was connected with the Baptists), and the members all knowing of the change that had passed upon me, hailed me as a man that had repented of his sins, and believed in the Lord Jesus Christ, and wished me to be baptized, and to join the Church. Having first given myself to the Lord, I was willing to give myself also to them; but I was prejudiced against being baptized, and all the reasonings that man could reason would not have persuaded me. I experienced much anxiety, and even distress of mind, regarding this matter. I lost a whole night's sleep in endeavouring to find out whether adult baptism was agreeable to scripture, and sanctioned by the Lord Jesus. I spent the night in prayer to God, and in studying his word. At last I came to the conclusion, after a most careful and prayerful study of the subject, and whatever is *not* of faith is *sin*, and I reasoned thus with myself : When I was born, I was a weakly child, and thought not likely to live. My father, thinking it would endanger any chance I might have of life, took me to the church, sent for the minister to *sprinkle* me, and put up a prayer, and called it baptism. My father, as I am informed, being an unbeliever, thought, if I died, I should go to heaven, after being sprinkled. When, however, I became enlightened from above, I came to the conclusion that it was all sin together, because it was done in unbelief. My father was an unbeliever that held me up. I was an unbeliever, because I was born in sin, and was unconscious at the time of what was done to me, and the minister that christened me was a Moderate. He was the parish minister of Old Kilpatrick. He had a large farm near his church and manse, and although I wish to be charitable, I am afraid that he minded his farm more than he minded his flock. I read in the 8th of the Acts of the Apostles, that as Philip and the eunuch " went on their way, they came unto a certain water, and the eunuch said, See, here is water ; what doth hinder me to be baptized ? And Philip said, If thou believest with all thine heart, thou mayest. And he answered and said, I believe that Jesus Christ is the Son of God. And he commanded the chariot to stand still ; and they went down both into the water, both Philip and the eunuch, and he baptized him. And when they were come up out of the water, the spirit of the Lord caught away Philip,

that the eunuch saw him no more, and he went
on his way rejoicing" (Acts viii. 36-39).

I read also, that when Jesus commanded his
disciples to go and preach the gospel to every
creature, he added these words : "He that believeth and is baptized, shall be saved" (Mark
xvi. 16). Believing is here put before baptism,
and "without faith it is impossible to please
God" (Hebrews xi. 6). Jesus himself was
baptized in the river Jordan, and all the apostles,
and all the primitive Christians were baptized.
I was thus fully persuaded, in my own mind, that
adult baptism was in accordance with the word
of God, and that, if I loved him, I must obey his
commands cheerfully and believingly. So I gave
in my name to the church in the regiment, and
word was sent to the mission church in the city,
that Robert Flockhart had become a true penitent,
had repented of his sins, and through divine grace
had believed on the Lord Jesus Christ, and was
recommended to the church in Calcutta for baptism
and admission to membership.

A deep interest being felt by the brethren in
the regiment in my case, application was made
by them individually to their respective officers
for leave to go to Calcutta, distant from Fort-
William about three miles, to be present at my
baptism. Leave was granted, and I got up early
the following Sabbath morning and went to
church in the Bazaar. The service being ended,
the missionaries were kind enough to invite us to
their residence, and we spent the rest of the

morning in devotional exercises. After being thus occupied for the greater portion of the morning, breakfast was provided for all of us by the missionaries' wives. It was truly a most delightful and gratifying spectacle to see thirty converted soldiers sitting down together at the same table in love and unity, and the missionaries' wives serving us all with warm affection.

It made me ashamed of myself. My heart melted with tears of joy when I thought what I once was, and what company I once kept, and now what a change had taken place. It was like a little heaven below.

After breakfast we prayed, and we sang praises to God, and our minds were prepared and in a pleasant frame to hear the gospel preached. Mr Ward preached the sermon from 1 Tim. i. " According to the glorious gospel of the blessed God, which was committed to my trust." It was a delightful sermon. Then after the sermon there were four persons to be baptized ; a civilian and his wife (the civilian was a white man, and his wife a coloured woman) a native woman, and the soldier—the red-coat. Two lines of a hymn were sung by each.

I shall never forget my two lines—

> " He was immersed in Jordan's flood,
> Then immersed in sweat and blood."

I saw in my baptism a lively representation of Christ's death, burial and resurrection.

After the baptisms were over, the civilian and I went into a private room adjoining the church to change our dress. While doing so, he said to me, "How light I feel now after having performed this duty in a manner agreeable to God's word." Having resumed our usual clothing, we next went to commemorate the Lord's death, along with our brethren. Seated at the Lord's table for the first time, I had faith to discern the Lord's body broken for me, and his blood shed for me. By faith I ate his body, and drank his blood, and in doing so, he made himself "known" to me in the "breaking of bread." By the "ear of faith" I seemed to hear him saying, "Eat, O friends, and drink abundantly, O beloved!" I said in my heart, "O Lord God, this is not after the manner of men!" The more of his glory I saw, the lower I lay, and I was convinced that whatever I was or hoped to be, I owed it all to sovereign grace and redeeming love.

Many have carnal views of the Lord's supper. They look no farther than the bread and wine. Faith, however, looks at Christ and lives upon him.

If I had life before, that life required to be nourished, so that I could not have fed on Him, if I had not had life before coming to the ordinance. I was surprised when I came to Edinburgh, and heard ministers stating to crowded congregations that the Lord could not die, and mystifying what is (already) a great mystery, viz., that "God was manifest in the flesh, as the sinner's representative to do and to suffer all that law, and truth, and justice required. No mere man or angel could do this, and he must be the Son of God, in our nature, who could. His actual obedience was called the righteousness of God. His passive obedience satisfied Divine justice, magnified the law, and made it honourable. Christ God as well as man, in two distinct natures, and one person for ever. Hence the apostle, writing to the Corinthians, says, in reference to this wondrous fact— "Howbeit we speak the wisdom of God in a mystery, even the hidden wisdom which God ordained before the world unto our glory, which none of the princes of this world knew, for had they known it they would not have crucified the Lord of glory." The apostle declares again, "That no man can say that Jesus is the Lord, but by the Holy Ghost." Elsewhere he says, "The life which I now live in the flesh, I live by the faith of the Son of God, who loved me, and gave himself for me." In Matthew we read, that when Jesus asserted that he was the Son of God, the Jews said he "blasphemed" (chap. xxvi. 63-65).

The incarnation of the Son of God is a mystery into which the "angels desire to look" (1 Peter i. 12). The redeemed around the throne of God will also be continuing to dive into this great mystery, but without ever getting thoroughly to the bottom of it, through all eternity. And the reason of this is, because the finite can never comprehend and grasp the infinite. The redeemed will ever sing "unto him that loved us, and washed us in his own blood;" and though their knowledge will be ever growing, ever increasing, it will ever continue to be a new song throughout all eternity. Oh what a deep stain sin has made on our nature, that nothing but divine blood could wash it out of the soul! (See Acts xx. 28).

"Forasmuch as ye know that ye were not redeemed with corruptible things such as silver and gold, but with the precious blood of Christ, as of a lamb without blemish and without spot" (1 Pet. i. 18, 19).

Whoever may read what I have written may think me very strange, but I cannot help it. My guilty conscience was fully awakened, and my spirit wounded—the sword of God's law was hanging over my head and my sins set in order before me, and the devil was tempting me to despair. What gave me relief but faith in that blood of which we have been speaking, when applied by the Spirit of God? This pacified my guilty conscience, removed the guilt from my heart, healed my afflicted mind, and gave me peace.

But to return. After the agreeable meeting with God's children in the morning, and hearing the sweet sermon, and the baptism and the Lord's supper were over, one of the office-bearers of the church kindly invited me to go and ride along with him in his chariot to his house, and there dine with him. His house stood about half way between Fort William and Calcutta, and he was governor of the jail at that place. On consideration, however, I decided to refuse his friendly offer. I was but a

young convert—my conscience was tender—I was
afraid he would ask me to drink ; that was my
reason, and I was afraid of falling into sin. I
was a " brand plucked out of the fire," and a
brand, unlike a green stick, is easily rekindled.
So I determined to decline the invitation, and
went home to my own house rejoicing. The path
of duty is the path of safety.

Speaking of my baptism, and the proceedings
connected with it, I may observe that Mr Ward,
who baptized me, said he had not spent a happier
day since he left England. Mr Carey was not
present on the occasion, being busily occupied
with his own work at Serampore, which was, the
translating and printing of the Scriptures in the
different languages spoken by the people of India.
Before leaving this subject, I may inform the
reader that my baptism took place on the 26th of
August 1810, and that an account of it is given
in the Baptist periodical, "No. 20," in which my
name is mentioned among others. Encouraged
by their success, the missionaries now came more
frequently to the barracks than before, although
forbidden by the officers. They used to come and
breakfast with the men, on which occasions they
always endeavoured to improve the opportunity,
like our blessed Lord among the Pharisees, and
publicans, and sinners. The soldiers used to say,
" We won't give ourselves up as yet, when such
good men come amongst us, who are such bad
characters." Some people found fault with me
because I spoke to the harlots in the street, and

went among the outcasts in the jail ; but these were just the sort of people our Lord himself went among. Publicans and harlots will enter into the kingdom of heaven before the self-righteous.

AFTER making a public profession of religion, I enjoyed sweet fellowship with the brethren in the regiment. Our love to one another resembled that of the Christian Church after the day of Pentecost. I used to experience great delight in meeting with two or three of the Christian brethren for prayer and praise behind a battery. Some of the ungodly soldiers found out our place of meeting, and sent in showers of stones among us ; but in place of terrifying us, it only made us more earnest to come back again, and the fire of grace and love burn more bright and warm.

About this time Mr Chamberlain and his wife, of whom I have already spoken, came up the river to preach the gospel at the different mission-stations in connection with the Church. They proceeded in a large boat, called a budgerow, drawn by natives employed for the purpose. They halted at Burhampore, and some of the brethren (converted soldiers), who had a great love for him, went down to salute him as he was passing up the river, and completely filled his boat. Mrs Chamberlain came upon deck and saluted the brethren (who unable to get on board the budgerow, were standing on the river's bank), saying, "There is no more room in the boat for you, but there is room for you all in my heart."

After that we did not remain long in Fort-William, as an order came for us to set out, in company with several other regiments, on an expedition to take the Isle of France. A number of lighters were provided to convey us down the river to Diamond Harbour. These lighters, filled with soldiers, proceeded out to a deeper part of the river, where larger vessels were stationed to receive us. On entering the boat to carry me, I happened to turn my head to see what was going on, and the first object that caught my eye was a corporal (well known to me) seated at the bow of the boat. The small boat at that moment struck the larger one, and suddenly I saw him fall backwards into the river, and, notwithstanding he made great struggling, he was borne rapidly down the stream. Although surrounded with boats, somehow or other he could not be rescued, and he soon sank to rise no more. I daresay I could have saved him, as I was an expert swimmer, had I jumped instantly into the water after him, but in the confusion and amazement of the moment my presence of mind forsook me—a dark horror seized on my soul. That man was one of my most violent persecutors. As soon as he perceived the great change that had been wrought upon me, I suffered hot persecution from him. I bore it patiently, although he had told me that he "would do for me." We had to sail a considerable way down the river before we got to Diamond

Harbour, where the transports were lying that were to carry us to the Isle of France. These vessels were as large as seventy-fours. When we got on board, each soldier got a hammock and blanket for himself. I well remember the very agreeable sensation I experienced when swinging from side to side with the motion of the ship. In the morning the boatswain sounded his whistle, and gave the word, "All hands up hammocks!" This was the signal for a "general rising" throughout the ship. As soon as we were all out of bed, the boatswain or his mate saw the hammocks stowed in the netting round the sides of the ship, so that we were all in readiness for the French if they should come in the way.

The hammocks were stowed away three or four deep round the sides of the ship, and acted as a defence against the shot of the enemy. If a strange sail came in sight during the night, the boatswain would instantly give the signal, "down chests and up hammocks!" Then the commodore would immediately signal the frigates that accompanied us, and formed part of our convoy, to go off and see whether the strange sail was a friend or a foe. The moment the frigates got the order, up went top-gallant sails, sky-scrapers, moon-rakers, and studding-sails, and off they flew, a beautiful sight to see, like birds on the wing! As soon as the strange sail had come sufficiently near, the captain would hail her through his speaking-trumpet, and say, "What ship? Where are you bound for? What's your cargo!" and, by the answers he got, he would know whether she was a friend or a foe. If she was a friend, up went the friendly signal; if a foe, then the signal was, "Prepare for action." Happily we met with no obstruction during the whole voyage from Diamond Harbour to the Isle of France, which we reached in about six weeks after leaving Calcutta. We had a very pleasant voyage, and the church assembled together for worship in the ship, and we earnestly prayed that the Lord would be pleased to cover our heads in the battle, and grant us the victory; that he would bestow skill and foresight on our commander, and grant strength and courage to ourselves, and success to our enterprise, at as small a sacrifice of human life as possible. This prayer was heard and answered, as the reader will learn afterwards.

During our passage we were rather scarce of water. I remember we had a sheet of canvas spread over our heads to protect us from the burning heat of the sun. When the rain fell, this sheet was filled with water, which we gladly and thankfully made use of. The serjeant-major found fault with me for doing so. Being very thirsty at the time (as I was living on salt provisions, and suffering severely from the want of water, having none even to make tea), I was really impudent to him, at the same time obeying his orders. "Serjeant-major, do you find fault with me for making use of what God sends down to us from heaven? Do you not remember when you sent for me to come and pray with you when you had the cramp in your stomach?" He made no reply.

Well might the Psalmist say, that "they that go down to the sea in ships, that do business in great waters; these see the works of the Lord, and his wonders in the deep." I have seen, with my own eyes, a cloud sent down by the Lord, in the middle of which there was, as it were, a dark pillar —this is the water-spout. Its appearance is usually preceded by a small dark cloud, such as was seen by the servant of Elija in the first book of Kings xviii. 44. These literal things have all a spiritual meaning. I could myself explain and illustrate them in my own way; but as the readers of these lines may have better abilities for the task than I can pretend to, I will only mention two.

Whilst I was in the Cape of Good Hope, a water-spout burst upon Table Hill, and inundated a great part of Cape-Town. At Castle Advance, the men on guard had to leave the lower floor of the guard-house, and ascend to the roof to save themselves from being drowned. There were many drowned by the deluge produced by this water-spout else-where throughout the town. "Deep calleth unto deep at the noise of thy water-spouts; all thy waves and thy billows are gone over me." These water-spouts, however, of the Psalmist's, were of a different description from those I have been describing. The deep sufferings endured by the Lord Jesus Christ call for deep sorrow for the sin which caused them. It is well known that all the waters we have in rivers and ponds come out

of the sea. As Solomon says, "All the rivers run
into the sea : yet the sea is not full : Unto the
place from whence the rivers come, thither they
return again." So all true grace comes from the
ocean above. God himself is the fountain of
living waters ; and while Adam, by his fall, shut
up the gate of heaven against himself and all his
posterity, Jesus Christ, by his active and passive
obedience, chiefly in Gethsemane and on Calvary,
and by his resurrection and ascension to the right
hand of the Father, threw it open again to all his
faithful followers ; and the holy Spirit, the Third
Person of the Trinity, applies the blessings Christ
has purchased by his death and sufferings to the
souls of believers.

> "Eternal Spirit, we confess
> And sing the wonders of thy grace ;
> Thy power conveys our blessings down
> From God the Father, and the Son."

To continue the simile : What God bestows he
requires back again, like the sea, with usury.
Paul says he did not receive the grace of God in
vain. "He laboured more abundantly than all
the apostles." Again, in Corinthians, he repeats
this expression, and says, "Yet not I, but the grace
of God which was with me."

I now come back to the expedition to the Isle
of France. . I may mention that we had two commanders, General Abercrombie, and another
General whose name I now forget. The object of
our commanders was to take the place with the
loss of as few lives as possible ; and this object, in

consequence of their skilful measures, they attained,
thus verifying the truth of the wise king's state-
ment:—" Every purpose is established by counsel;
and with good advice make war " (Prov. **xx.** 18).
The harbour of Port Louis is surrounded with
mountains; the entrance to it is narrow, and
across this entrance the enemy had stretched a
boom or chain. There was, however, a narrow
passage by which the harbour might be entered
unknown to the enemy. This passage no person
knew but the pilot. They bribed the pilot to lead
in our men-of-war. As soon as our ships got in,
they formed in line of battle in front of Port
Louis, and opened their ports. The seamen
manned the guns, and threw in their balls and
bombshells. Whilst our ships of war were thus
employed in diverting the attention of the enemy,
the transports were engaged in landing the troops
at the back of the island, which they did, and
that too in the middle of the day, and without any
opposition. We then marched off towards the
town, and did not halt till it was dark. The
most of us had a little rest upon the ground. We
lay with our loaded firelocks in our bosoms.
After we had slept a little while, an alarm was
given that the enemy was coming. I woke
out of my sleep very confused, but soon Lieutenant-Colonel Dalrymple, who commanded the
22d regiment, told us we might go to sleep again,
for it was a false alarm.

As soon as it was day, we set out again on our
march, the sharp-shooters in front, and proceeded

right onwards till we came up to the French batteries, which instantly opened on us with grape and round shot. We did not stop to pop, pop at them, but made a charge, and drove them from their guns. Down went the French colours, up went the British flag; with a huzza we went after them. At this period of the engagement I fell in with a tub of water, which had been left behind by some Madagascar slaves who had been at work in the field. Very thirsty, I knelt down to get a drink from it. Scarcely had I, with others, quenched my thirst and bathed my face, when up came Colonel Dalrymple, and capsized the tub. "How do you know," said he, "but that the enemy may have poisoned the water?" That thought never struck me at the time, I was so thirsty. I may observe that it is even hotter in the Isle of France than in Bengal, so that one is more liable to be thirsty, if it were possible, there, than in India. Towards night it began to rain very heavily; and the greater number of the men being completely wearied out, half of the army lay down on the ground, liberty having been given by the Generals, and slept turn about. I lay down in the open field. Strange to say, though I had only the bare ground to lie on, and a stone for my pillow, and the rain continued to fall heavily, I slept as soundly as if I had been lying on a feather bed. I remember, also, that it rained heavily on our soldiers the night before the battle of Waterloo, although I was not there, and I understand that it rained heavily on our brave fellows the first day they set foot on the Crimea. After taking the batteries, as already mentioned, and blowing up a magazine that supplied them, we marched right on to Port Louis. On our appearance before the town, the garrison opened a heavy fire of round shot, grape, and bombshells upon us.

The wounded lay groaning on every side of us. I observed a French soldier lying on his face at a short distance from me, with his clothes on fire. Stepping hastily out of the ranks, I ran up to him. I said to myself, "Poor fellow, I will put the fire out, and take him aside if he is alive." Turning him over on his back, I saw that he was dead. I let him lie, and hurried back to my place in the ranks. The balls at this moment were flying thick around me, and over me, and ploughing up the ground before me. They were flying over my head just the same as when boys play at ball. An unseen hand, however, shielded me, and threw them over my head. There is no truer saying than that "every bullet has its billet," let men think what they will. Of that I myself am a living witness. Ahab disguised himself at Ramoth-Gilead, but his disguise protected him not; for a certain man drew a bow at a venture, and smote him between the joints of his harness ; and, as for David, he confesses, "Thou hast covered my head in the day of battle."

During the whole time my mind was in a praying frame. I expected every moment would be my last. I never lived nearer the Lord than at

that time. Lifting up my voice, I sang the
following stanza :—

> ".Plagues and death around me fly,
> Till he bid, I cannot die ;
> Not a single shaft can hit,
> Till the God of love sees fit."

This verse I also repeated—

> " When I tread the verge of Jordan,
> Bid my anxious fears subside ;
> Death of Death, and hell's destruction,
> Land me safe on Canaan's side,
> Songs of praises I will ever give to thee."

At this time General Sir Ralph Abercrombie and
the other General, wishing to prevent the loss of
life as much as possible, and to save their men,
commanded the bugler to sound a retreat. So we
retired till nearly out of the range of the enemy's
shot. The British commanders then sent a
message under a flag of truce, to the French
commander, threatening to lay the town in ashes
if he did not submit, and ground his arms. This
we could easily have done, as the houses were
built of wood. At that time there was an
awkward fellow on guard. He saw some of our
men walking about at night, and fired on them,
and they fired on us. The officer on guard cried
out, " Men, cease, you are shooting our own men ! "
The French General submitted to the terms pro-
posed, and yielded himself and his men prisoners
of war.

This was brought about, I understand, by the
leading citizens of Port Louis, who, it is said,
bribed their General to capitulate ; and I am of

opinion that there were grounds for the suspicion, because a large quantity of gold was afterwards discovered on board the ship that was to convey him to France, and transferred from thence to the store-house, under an escort of our soldiers. At all events he surrendered, and he and his men were transmitted as prisoners of war to France, to be exchanged for other prisoners. This was in the year 1811. I myself and some others saw some vineyards without an owner. We went in and got some fruit, and honey from a bee-hive. That put me in mind of Samson's riddle—the lion was killed, and we got honey.

After the French had left the island, the brethren in the different regiments determined to meet together to return thanks to Almighty God for covering our heads in the day of battle, and giving us the victory. At the close of our quiet meeting, we commemorated the Lord's death in a beautiful field, on the green grass. A white cloth was spread on the sward for the bread and wine, around which we seated ourselves in a ring. Then pastor and office-bearers were placed in the middle. We sang the praises of God with a grateful heart. Then the pastor delivered an address, in which he spiritualised the events peculiar to the life of a soldier. "We have," he said, "other battles to fight besides those which we fight for our king and country. We have to fight against sin, and Satan, and the flesh, and there is no discharge from this war." Whilst listening to these remarks of the pastor, our minds, I trust, were led

by the Holy Spirit to that blessed time when the
Church militant shall be changed into the Church
triumphant, and when all who have loved the
Lord Jesus upon earth shall be admitted to behold his glory in heaven, and, seated at a table
never to be withdrawn, shall partake of the
marriage supper of the Lamb.

In that hot climate the nights are generally
very beautiful. The evening of the day on which
we commemorated the death of our Lord was
remarkably so. On that occasion the Lord Jesus
manifested himself, and was present with us. As
for my part, I had that promise fulfilled to my
experience; he made himself "known to me in
the breaking of bread." He breathed on me, and
said, "Receive ye the Holy Ghost." He feasted
our souls with his flesh, and gave us his blood to
drink, and said, "Eat, O friends; yea, drink
abundantly, O beloved!" I remember that night
with great delight; many of us had a foretaste
of heaven. The heavenly calm, the holy and
reverential awe, and profound humility, and the
sweet refreshment on his dying love, can never be
forgotten, coming, as they did, after the hair-
breadth escapes that we made from the messengers
of death, which mowed down men both on the
right hand and on the left.

After this the Lord again saw meet to lay his
rod upon me. I took the cramp in the stomach,
and reported myself sick to the doctor under
whom I had been a patient for two years at
Burhampore, as I formerly mentioned. On this

the doctor replied, "Robert, I can do no more
for you; you are to do no more duty. I will
have you invalided the first time the Board sits."
An officer who belonged to the same company as
that I belonged to, and whom I shaved every
morning, hearing of my interview with the doctor,
asked me what he said to me. I informed him,
and he said to me, "I'll tell you what to do; go
and take a bathe every morning in the sea." I
followed his directions, praying to God for a blessing on the means I was about to employ for the
recovery of my health. Accordingly, going down
to the sea, and taking off my clothes, I plunged
into the water, and it was blessed to me, for I
experienced benefit every time. By-and-by the
effects of the bathing became so apparent that
the men saw the improvement it made on me, and
said, "Robert is as well, and as able to do his
duty, as any of us." "Well," said I, "put me
on the roll, and I will do my duty again." And
so I did.

One day, shortly after this, I was ordered to
mount guard on a high hill where there were
some large guns that used to fire on us. They
planted me as sentry at a distance from the guard-
house, in a sequestered place, where I could meditate, and pray, and sing to the Lord. As I was
walking backwards and forwards at my post in
the wood, I began to praise God, and, I believe,
if ever I sang with the spirit and with the understanding, it was on this occasion. Suddenly a
multitude of angels joined in chorus with me.

Such heavenly music I never heard—no, nor ever will, till I arrive in heaven. Just as I ceased singing, a corporal and a sentry came to relieve me at my post, saying I must go before the Board and be examined. Accordingly I presented myself before the doctors, praying at the same time, like Nehemiah, silently. The head doctor made me uncover my breast; it was a little swollen. This proceeded from the medicine I had used whilst in hospital at Burhampore. The head doctor said I was a young man, and well able to do my duty. On this, my own doctor in the regiment, whose name was Doctor Hicken, said I had been a long time under his care. Immediately a rap came to the door of the Board-room; it was opened; some great man wished to speak to the head doctor, who went out to him accordingly. As soon as he was gone out, Dr Hicken, the next in seniority after the head doctor, put me down as unfit for service. That was an answer to my prayer; that was what the singing was for. The Lord had determined to bring me away from that place, as he had other work for me elsewhere.

Before leaving the Isle of France, I wish to give a description of the place, and the manners of the people. In the first place, I may mention that thirty of our merchant ships, which had been captured by the enemy, were lying in the harbour. There were also in Port Louis a number of prisoners from the 24th regiment, some of whom joined the French, and fought against us. After the taking of the island, these men fell into our hands, and they were tried and sentenced to be hanged on a tree.

With regard to the moral conduct of the inhabitants, I believe that the fear of God was not in all the island. It is said in Scripture, "by their fruits shall ye know them." The French had a number of Madagascar slaves to work for them. These poor creatures were cruelly treated by the French. They were compelled to work every day in the year. The only day of rest they had was Christmas. They were punished very cruelly. An iron collar was placed around the neck of the slave. Sometimes three or four spikes were fastened to the collar to prevent him (or her) from getting any rest when lying down. Two men and two women were chained together, and made to drag carts like horses. I have seen some of these slaves that were chained to the anvil, others of them chained to the vice-board, and others again to a place in the wall to blow the fire. After the taking of the island, the British, on the Sabbath, hoisted the royal flag, as a signal that divine service was to begin. These services were conducted in the same manner as in the Church of England. The government provided a chaplain for every regiment, who read prayers, and the soldiers made the responses to them. This external profession had its effect upon the people of the island, and made them think and enquire.

In consequence of my remaining so short a time

in the island (only half-a-year), I am unable to give a very full account of it. Before leaving the place, I may mention that it was left to my discretion to go to the battle-field or to the sick-ship. I resolved, in the strength of the Lord, to go to the field of battle, lest I should injure the cause of religion by the ungodly saying that my religion had made me a coward. I would rather have died first, than bring disgrace upon the cause of Christ. Those who knew me since will not have any doubt of this. I swore to be loyal to my king and country; and I was always a good soldier. And in proof of this I may mention that I afterwards got both pension and prize-money in the Veteran battalion, as I will relate by-and-by. I observed the mysterious hand of God in the providence that took me out of the regiment at this time, as we were ordered to the island of Bourbon. The island is distant about 100 miles from the Isle of France. I am informed that the regiment was greatly broken up after I left it, and stationed in separate companies in different parts of the island. In consequence of this, the church suffered severely, and was exposed to many persecutions and temptations to sin, and I heard a bad account of many who had once made professions. The Lord, however, brought me out before that, and sent the serjeant of the hospital along with me. I experienced the truth of the old saying on my voyage to England, that "two are better than one." The serjeant had been discharged on account of a sore leg, which incapacitated him from doing certain things for himself, which I could do for him. I therefore thought it my duty to save him, as much as possible, from any toil or labour I could perform in his stead. I did this out of love to him, and to prove my gratitude to him for permitting me to come and join him in family worship. Moreover, it was during my early intercourse with him that I found peace. During the voyage, each soldier was required to take down his hammock, lash it up, and bring it upon deck every morning, and to carry it down again at night. The boatswain, or boatswain's mate, piped every morning, "Up all hammocks!" This signal was followed by a second, to "Stow them in the netting," where they remained during the day. At night they were taken down again with the same ceremonies. Now, these friendly offices I performed for the serjeant—taking down, and lashing up, and carrying on deck his hammock along with my own.

There were six men in our mess; they took the duties of "orderly" in succession, one at a time. I took his "orderly" as well as my own—carrying the mess, and performing the customary duties. We used to have worship regularly every day by ourselves. This made the voyage pleasant, kept grace in lively exercise, and inclined us to seek for more grace out of Christ's fulness, from whence we had received it at first. There is a beautiful passage bearing on this subject in Phil. i. 19,— "For I know that this shall turn to my salvation through your prayer, and the supply of the spirit of Jesus Christ." "Whatsoever things were written aforetime were written for our learning; that we through patience and comfort of the Scriptures might have hope" (Rom. xv. 4). Whenever I used to feel my mind not so comfortable as I could wish, I went to a quiet place for self-examination and prayer; and where was this but at the bowsprit, in a cradle that holds the jib-sail, with the sea under me, and the lightning flashing around me in the firmament. I often found this exercise profitable; it recalled to my mind my "former ways." David did the same, he says:—

> "I thought upon my former ways,
>   And did my life well try;
>   And to thy testimonies pure
>     My feet then turned I." PSALM cxix. 59.

This exercise, also, had a tendency to keep me humble, and gave me matter for confession and earnest prayer, and produced in my heart more love to God for looking upon such a vile sinner as I had been. I knew and felt that I deserved to be cast into the ocean of God's wrath for ever, and to have the lightnings of his anger beating on my naked soul, throughout eternity. I have no tongue to express my gratitude to him for what he has done and suffered, to save me from the lowest and hottest hell! How can I show it? What would I not do or suffer for him who has done and suffered so much for me? Alas, after all I can do, I am but an unprofitable servant!

I can never forgive myself for spending the cream of my life in the service of the devil, till I was twenty-nine years of age. Since the Lord, however, has been pleased to call me effectually, I have endeavoured to serve him to the utmost of my feeble ability. Still, I must admit that sin is mingled with all I do, even with my best services, to this very day. The sins of my holy things are none of the least of my sins. Alas, alas, how often have I sinned against the clearest light, the tenderest love, and the most amazing long-suffering and mercy! But to return to my voyage.

At length we came in sight of St Helena, a huge rock in the middle of the ocean, far from any land, accessible only on one side, and so very lofty that it can be descried at a distance of sixty miles. When we reached St Helena, we found about thirty transports and large merchantmen lying at anchor. Being the time of war, every ship had a number of cannons on board, besides a powder magazine and sufficient shot. During the time we lay at anchor, the king's birthday (the 4th of June) arrived. At twelve or one o'clock, every ship fired a royal salute of twenty-one guns. The effect produced by the united thunder of thirty broadsides may be imagined, but not described. The ship in which I was, happened to be lying in the middle of the fleet, and I was rendered deaf by the stunning noise for a considerable while after. When the ships had done firing, the batteries on the island commenced. The firing, I may observe, was a beautiful sight, as the guns were only a short distance from us, and rose, tier over tier, right above our heads. Whilst we lay at St Helena, I obtained permission to go on shore on two different occasions. As I had been living on salt provisions all the time I was on shipboard, I felt a desire to have a refreshment of savoury meat, at a house of entertainment on the island. On obtaining what I wanted, I followed the example of Abraham, who erected an altar to God wherever he went, and asked the blessing of the Lord on the food he had provided for my body, and praised and thanked him for that which he had already provided for my soul, even the bread of life (oh, the rich food!) that "comes down from heaven."

Little did I think that this was the place where Buonaparte was to be a prisoner for life, and where, at length, he was "to cease from troubling." How mysteriously does God in his providence arrange all his purposes, catching those haughty monarchs in their own nets, to manifest his glory. I remark, I never saw so many fish as I saw at the place where we lay at anchor, at the rock at St Helena. The small fish were on the surface of the water, and were numberless, and the deeper you go, the fish are larger. There being a little boat alongside the ship, having a hook and line, I went down into it, and cast my hook into the sea, and caught many. There is a pleasure in fishing where there are many, and it is easy to catch them. So it is with ministers when they have a great congregation; they take a pleasure in the prospect that their labour will be blessed to win souls to Christ. Oh! that he would bid his fishermen cast the net at the right side of the ship, that they may find! Without that they will toil all the night of their life, and catch nothing.

We then set sail for England, and had a very pleasant passage. We disembarked at Chelsea, and I was very glad when I once more put my foot on British ground. Then, I went before the board to be inspected, with Sergeant Macfarlane. They discharged him, as he had a sore leg, and gave him a pension of a shilling a day; and they put me down for the 12th Veteran battalion, that lay in Youghal, in Ireland. I said to the board, "For what do you send me to Ireland? I am a Scotchman." They said, "We cannot alter now; we will give you a letter to the colonel of the 12th Veterans, who will write a memorial to the Duke of York, to get you into the 9th Veterans, lying in Edinburgh Castle."

I remained at Chelsea about six weeks, billeted in a respectable house. I chose for my company the people of God, and used to attend the public ordinances of religion, as a means of keeping the life of grace in my soul, which I felt always needed to be fed by Christ, in the use of his institutions. I remember walking in a large park in London, when in meditation and prayer, to my surprise I felt the wind blow upon my soul and body. It went through and through me, and made the very bones of my body to rejoice in the Lord, and it stirred up the graces of my soul, and gave them fresh life and vigour. I could exclaim with the Psalmist, in the 103d Psalm—"Bless the Lord, O my soul; and all that is within me, bless his holy name. Bless the Lord, O my soul, and forget not all his benefits; who forgiveth all thine iniquities; who healeth all thy diseases; who redeemeth thy life from destruction; who crowneth thee with loving kindness and tender mercies." The last verse of the 4th chapter of Canticles came into my mind—"Awake, O north wind; and come, thou south; blow upon my garden, that the spices thereof may flow out. Let my beloved come into his garden, and eat his pleasant fruits." This was not a fancy, but it was a reality; I say it to God's honour and glory. After what I have written in my life already about my bad life, it would be a sin were I now to hide God's kindness and goodness; for what he has done for my soul is all free, sovereign, unmerited favour from God in Christ to me, the chief of sinners—to me, who deserved the lowest hell; and I ascribe all the glory to a Three-One God. I connected myself with a Baptist church the time I was there, and having informed them that I was going to Ireland, some of the brethren got a bundle of religious tracts for me to circulate among the Irish. They could not have given me a better present; it was a delightful employment to be engaged in. Then a party of us was sent off to march to the Isle of Wight. We marched a good way from London till we came to an arm of the sea where we were to cross to the Isle of Wight;

but on our march from London we stopped a night, and the men were billeted in different houses, and to my surprise, my billet was in a disreputable house. The women all stared at me as I came in ; but I immediately took off my knapsack and haversack, in which I had some victuals. The landlord brought a table, on which I set my provisions. I was very hungry after my day's march, and after my usual manner of life, I asked a blessing before I partook. It came into my mind to make it a prayer for the good of the inmates, and to prevent the females from using any imprudence towards me while partaking of the meal ;—experimentally knowing the terrors of the Lord, I warned them to flee from the wrath to come, faithfully and impressively from my heart setting the horrors of hell before them. Their house was just the way to hell ; as Solomon, says in the proverbs—" Her house is the way to hell, going down to the chambers of death." It had an effect upon them ; while I was eating it seemed to bind them hand and foot. I gave them time to think before I brought comfort to them after I ate my meal. I thought to myself, the needle of the law makes way for the thread of the gospel ; so after my meal was over I returned thanks. I forget now my words ; but I used every means to open to them the door of escape, by showing them that it was just of such characters as they were, such as Rahab the harlot, and Mary Magdalene, that Jesus spoke when he said to the Pharisees, " The publicans and harlots go in to the kingdom of God before you." I left these words with them, and thought I was long enough there. "Escape for thy life!" Away I went to see my comrades, and to see if I could get a better billet. I asked a soldier that I knew, what kind of a billet he had got? He answered, "I have got a fine billet." Said I to him— "Would there be room for me?" "Yes, Robert, if you have got a bad billet, come beside me." That was just what I wanted. I went back to get my knapsack and other chattels, and carried them off in a hurry. The landlord of the house wanted me to stay; I said, "I am too long here; I would not sleep on the road to hell."

We went to the Isle of Wight, and I remained there, I think, about six weeks. I got information that there was a Baptist church, I think it was at Gosport, a place at a little distance from the Isle of Wight barracks, which is a great place for drafting young soldiers. I got acquainted with the minister and the members. We used to have social meetings together, and they sounded how I became religious in the army. I told them the same as I have stated in the foregoing pages. They seemed to be surprised, and broke out with this expression:—"Dear me, there is a man that was converted 15,000 miles from us, and has the same experience as ourselves;" and they concluded and said, "It is the work of the same Spirit." The time arrived that I must go and join the 12th Veterans. There were about 300 recruits to be sent aboard ship along with me to the Cove of

Cork. After we had set sail, there arose a tempestuous storm, and the ship drove in toward a place called Milford Haven, in Wales, where they cast anchor; but it was bad anchorage ground, and the ship dragged till we got very near a high rock. They said all hope of being saved was lost. There were none of the soldiers allowed to go on deck. There was a sort of horror seized my mind, and I went on deck, and looked up to the big, black, stormy clouds, and down to the mountainous waves, and to the high rocks we were just going against, and the ship dragging her anchor. I darted a prayer up to heaven in the name of the Lord Jesus, and looked for an answer; as it was the time of my extremity, it might be the time of the Lord's opportunity. I said, "O Lord, I am not worthy that thou shouldst hear or answer my prayer; but answer the prayers of the people that I was amongst that prayed for me—I mean the church at Gosport." The reason of this was, that in all my voyages I always encountered terrible storms, and was nearly lost. Immediately after the prayer was put up, the anchor held, and terror fled from my mind, and I went down amongst the soldiers; and what were they doing but telling stories and tales to drive the terror of death from their minds. I spoke to them like a man that had authority from the Lord that answered prayer:— "That is pretty conduct; you should have been upon your knees, confessing your sins, with grief in your heart, and tears in your eyes, crying, 'God be merciful to me a sinner.'" I preached Jesus

to them, and " him crucified," and they heard me
with the greatest attention. I told them to be of
good cheer, the anchor held, and they should not
be lost. That night I observed one of the soldier's
wives praying with tears in her eyes; the next
day the weather became fine, and I heard that
woman curse. I said to her, " You were praying
last night, and you are cursing to-day; what a
contradiction! The terrors of your mind fled
when the storm was over, and now you are offending the same God that saved you from being
drowned, and perishing in the waters."

Being a fine day, we weighed anchor, and set
off for the Cove of Cork. We disembarked there,
and I marched to Youghal, where the 12th Veteran
battalion lay, and I delivered the letter to the
Colonel about my desire to go to Scotland. The
rest of the recruits went to their different regiments, and the Lord gave me favour in the eyes
of the Colonel and all the officers. The Colonel
ordered the Adjutant to write a memorial to the
Duke of York, requesting that I might go to a
veteran battalion in Scotland. I was nearly two
months with the 12th regiment in Youghal. The
Duke of York granted my request, that I should
be sent to the 9th Veteran battalion that lay in
Edinburgh Castle. The Duke was a good soldier's
friend. However, during the time I was there, I
connected myself with a religious body of Christians. The minister I loved dearly; he preached
sound doctrine, and all the members of his church
seemed like-minded. They had social meetings

and fellowship one with another. They read a chapter, and both male and female spoke from it, and we had prayer and praise. They did not despise me, though I had a red coat on. They invited me to their houses, and we talked one to another about the things that belong to our peace. It being a church where there were rich members, they made a conscience every week of collecting money for the poor. I said to the minister, " I want something to do ; have you nothing for me to do ? " He laughed with joy at my offer, and at once employed me to distribute the money, after giving me the addresses of every one I was to call on, and what I was to give to each ; and they could not give me better work. There was one house in particular I went to, where I saw an aged woman, about a hundred years of age, and a daughter of hers, about fourscore. It would have drawn pity from your heart to see the miserable condition they were in. They heard me with great attention. I read a chapter from the Word of God, and spoke to them, and told them there was only " one Mediator between God and men, the man Christ Jesus ; " and that it was faith in his finished work that justified the ungodly, and so on. In other houses I went to I would drive away the Pope, and penances and purgatory, in all directions, and I prayed with them, and they went on their knees with me, both men and women. There were swine walking about in their houses as large as hogs.

The members of that church were very zealous,

both ladies and gentlemen. They had a large school, and on the Sabbath-day they met in the church with the children in the middle of the day, between sermons, and heard them repeat their tasks. I was surprised to hear the children say their lessons so well. Some of them repeated a whole epistle that they learned by heart in the course of a week. I have seen many schools in Scotland; but Irish children in general, I have observed, are more ready to learn to read than the Scotch, and they have a good memory to retain what they learn.

So the time came that I was to leave, and I got my discharge, and marched from Youghal to Dublin; the distance, I believe, is 100 miles. I had authority to go to the billet-master to give me a billet for a night in any house he chose. I had a bundle of tracts with me in my knapsack, which I distributed by the way. On one occasion I saw a group of Irishmen together, and finding that four of them could read, I offered to make them a present of a tract. One man was eager to receive it, and, standing up, he read it to all that were there, and they heard it with attention. We in Scotland think lightly of a tract, but they thought it was a great gift indeed. When I went a little further, I fell in with a packman. I asked him what he had to sell, and he opened his pack and showed me a lot of pictures. They were pictures of the saints; the Virgin Mary was one of them, and St Peter, and many others. I told him if he would give me the pictures I would give him

tracts for them, and he would get more for the
tracts than the pictures ; he willingly exchanged,
and went away. What I got I disposed of in this
way : having reached a place where no person
saw me, I tore up the saints, and buried them in
a field. I hope that all the mischief they could
do was buried with them.

When I got a billet in any house, I sat up till
bed-time to see if they had any devotions, and
with great grief I saw and heard them worshipping they knew not what—praying to the Virgin
Mary and the rest of the departed saints to inter-
cede for them ; there was no end to their applica-
tions. I was very civil, and did not interrupt
till they had done. Then I said to them, "You
will have no objection to permit me to worship
the Lord in the way that is revealed in his word?"
I took out the Bible, and first sang a few verses
of a psalm ; then I read a chapter that condemned
the manner in which they worshipped, showing
that there is only "one God, and one Mediator
between God and men, the man Christ Jesus,"
and that only through him we have "access by
one Spirit unto the Father." Then I went on my
knees, and down with their Popery, and up with
Christ, fearlessly, not regarding my life. I used
all means that I thought were calculated to lead
them the right way, knowing the value of their
souls, and that they were on the brink of a dreadful eternity. They looked at me with wonder,
and did me no harm, and then I went to bed.

This was the way I spent my time, as far as I

recollect, till I got to Dublin. Many I met on the road, and they would salute me with " God bless you !" This saying is common in Ireland, and is similar to our " Good day" in Scotland. In the Cape of Good Hope the salutation is " Ram, ram," and in India, in paying respect with the hand, it is " Salaam, sahib, salaam." " Sahib " is "master." If it is a poor person, and something is given him that he wants, he will go down on his knees, with great respect, and kiss your feet. The keepers of elephants ride on the necks of the animals, and speak to them in the Hindoo language, and teach them to beg. The elephant will come to you, and if you give it a piece of money, it takes it up with the end of its trunk, and hands it up to its keeper. He teaches the elephant to salute with a salaam those who give it a coin, and it lifts up its trunk and touches its head most respectfully. An elephant is the wisest creature I ever knew.

I arrived at head-quarters at Dublin, and having a letter from the Colonel of the 12th Veteran battalion, I delivered it. I remained there for some weeks, and during that time I became acquainted with many of the people of God. One gentleman invited a party of Christians, and me with them, to take breakfast. After we had all sat down, I was surprised with astonishment; they never asked a blessing before they began to partake. I did not know what to do or say, but I asked one silently to the Lord. It lay heavy on my mind when I was taking my breakfast, and

I found I must tell them that Jesus himself showed the example, and left that example in his Word that we might follow his steps, that whether we eat, or drink, or whatever we do, we may do all to the glory of God. I reasoned with them in a kind way and manner, not to offend them. They said to me, "As we omitted to ask God's blessing before we began, we will give you the honour to return God thanks when we have done;" and so I did. I did not spare one, in confessing our sins. When we were graceless, I said, we used to eat and drink to ourselves, and never gave God thanks; now that we profess to be his people, we are to be distinguished from what we once were, and from the people of the world; we are to acknowledge God in all our ways, and he shall direct our paths. They took it all very kindly, and we parted in good friendship.

The time came that I was to set off for Edinburgh Castle. There was a vessel bound for Irvine, and I had to go by her. In all my voyages, I had been in danger of being lost, but this last one, from Dublin to Irvine, was the pleasantest I ever had. In my mind, I compared it to my spiritual voyage, from my first outset in a natural state to my complete sanctification. I have had a rough passage to the haven that shall end my voyage. Now, as I am drawing near the end of my journey, I have so much of the gracious presence of my blessed Lord and Master, that my latter end seems to me to be better than the beginning; my evidence in my experience is

clearing up, and I have foretastes of that fulness
of joy which is reserved for them that are good
and faithful servants, and I ascribe all to the good
pleasure and sovereign grace of God in Christ
Jesus our Lord, and to Father, Son, and Holy
Ghost, one God, be all the glory !

We landed at Irvine at night.   I was billeted
in a decent house, and got up early in the
morning for my journey to Glasgow.   It is remarkable that the first church I was in in Scotland
was at Irvine.   In looking at it the first time I
set foot on Scottish ground, I could not express
the joy that sprang up in my heart.   How different I was when I left !   The Lord now seemed to
say, " This is the lot of your inheritance."   In his
kind purposes and gracious providence he had
brought me back, for my own good, and that I
might be instrumental in doing good to others.

Near Irvine, I fell in with a mason going to his
work in the morning, and he went along the road
a good way with me.   We got into religious conversation, and I found out that he was a real
Christian.   He and I went on our way rejoicing.
I believe from my heart that the Lord, who appeared to the disciples going to Emmaus, and
expounded to them the Scriptures, was graciously
and spiritually present with us.   We could say,
" Did not our heart burn within us while he
talked with us by the way ? "   I felt my heart
melted with love to the Lord Jesus, and he seemed
to feel the same.   He looked at me with astonishment, seeing a red coat on my back, and a knap-

sack on my shoulders. He thought such a man could not exist in the army. When he came to the place where he was to work, he shook hands with me, and blessed the Lord that he could have his people in any station of life. He took a shilling out of his pocket, and requested me to take it; but I refused. He was determined I should have it, and when I would not take it out of his hand, he laid it at my feet, and went away to his work. I thought it was better to lift it up than to let it be lost.

When I got to Glasgow, I went to the authorities, and told them I had a father and mother living in Old Kilpatrick, that I had not seen for fifteen years, and that I wished permission to go and see them. Kilpatrick is about ten miles west from Glasgow. They did not object; and having got my furlough lengthened for a couple more days, I went and saw my old father and mother. I had a young brother and two sisters staying with them. Two of my brothers were in the army, one in the 79th, the other in the 71st regiment. I had my red coat on, and my knapsack on my back. I was directed to my father's house. He lived up stairs one storey, and it was an outside stair that led to his house. My father was at the top of the stair and he saw me coming. He ran in and informed my mother and the rest of the family: "Here is Robert come home at last." After shaking hands, I requested that we should all go on our knees, and thank the Lord for his sovereign and gracious pleasure in sparing

us so long to see one another in the land of the
living, and in bringing me through so many
dangers ; and, above all, for what he had done for
my precious and immortal soul, and for letting
them see their son a different character from what
he was when he left them. They seemed to be
glad. After prayer, and a delightful conversation
together, the time came that I must set off to
join the 9th Veteran battalion. So I went to
Glasgow first, and from thence by coach to
Edinburgh. I was glad when I saw the old
Castle of Edinburgh.

I found out my regiment, and informed the
Adjutant of my translation from the 12th to the
9th Veterans, by order of the Duke of York, in
writing, and he ordered me to one of the old
barrack-rooms. Little did I think, when I went,
what was to follow. All the joy that I had formerly felt, was just preparing me for fiery trials.
I was landed among different men to what there
were in the 22d regiment. What a contrast ! I
was now amongst unreasonable and ungodly
sinners ; it seemed to me that the fear of God
was not before their eyes. They were like incarnate devils ; they had been at the wars, and
fought many battles, and they gloried in it. I
have observed of men that have done such exploits, that, if grace does not lay hold of them,
and subdue their ferocious spirit and raging and
murderous dispositions, they get hardened in
wickedness, and valiant in serving the devil and
their own lusts. I thought within myself, "How

can I serve God in a place like this?" I encouraged myself in the Lord, that as he had kept Lot in Sodom, he could keep me here. I began to think that I could perform the duties enjoined upon Christians secretly. I read my Bible in my berth; sometimes I would go behind the door to pray. There was one man in particular that watched my motions, and he came to me, and requested an interest in my prayers. A little after that, on a Sabbath morning, many of my comrades got up and cleaned their firelocks, and got their accoutrements ready for mounting guard, and they were whistling and singing, and cursing and swearing. I was lying in my bed awake, till I could stand it no longer. I knew it was no use speaking to them, as they were unreasonable, and would not hear me. I put on my greatcoat, and went into the middle of the barrack-room, and kneeled down at a form, lifting up my heart and my hand to God in heaven in prayer, telling him their conduct, and what a state sin had brought them to, and what a miserable life they lived, and the consequence of such a life, to endure God's wrath and curse in hell-fire for ever. My heart was broken and full of grief for their wickedness. I have been on the mighty ocean where the waves were swelling high, and I declare their conduct was just "like the troubled sea, when it cannot rest, whose waters cast up mire and dirt." I continued praying till they became dumb, and there was a calm in the barrack-room for a considerable time after that, just as when Jesus "rebuked the winds and the sea, and there was a great calm." I was obliged to live among them, and could say like David, "Oh that I had wings like a dove ; for then would I fly away and be at rest."

Another morning, soon after that, I got up out of my bed, and was putting on my greatcoat, when the Lord spoke to me. I heard the same words he spoke to Paul, as recorded in the Acts, "Be not afraid, but speak, and hold not thy peace : for I am with thee, and no man shall set on thee to hurt thee." "And thine ears shall hear a word behind thee." (Is. xxx. 21). I know few will believe it, but what I have to write is, that unless I had got that authority, I never could have been able to stand all the persecutions from men, and rage of devils, and discouragement from the people of God. But "I conferred not with flesh and blood." That is the account that I give for all the fortitude and courage that I had in obeying the command ; and if God had not commanded me, and sent me, I never should have spoken publicly in the streets, nor in the Castle among the soldiers. I would to God that every minister had the same assurance that he was sent by the Lord to preach the gospel as had that poor, unworthy, ignorant, and unlearned old veteran, Robert Flockhart. I do not say that this is God's general way to call men such as I am, but he taught me experimentally as he taught John Bunyan. God is not confined to fixed methods ; sometimes to accomplish his purpose he goes out of his usual way. When I mounted guard I reproved sin, and preached Christ and salvation from sin through his blood. I found by experience that it was the right way to separate me from their sinful conversation, and to bring me nearer to the Captain of my salvation. They used to watch my conduct, and would ask me questions, and seek to entangle me in my talk, but the Lord had blessed me with two ears, and only one tongue—" swift to hear, slow to speak "—I had to choose my words. I thought of the words, " We are of God : he that knoweth God heareth us ; he that is not of God heareth not us." It was very painful to my mind that they would make me as one of themselves, and I was no better, it was true, in one sense of the word : it was God that made the difference. By the grace of God I was different, and lived a different life from what they did, and from what I once did. We used to parade every morning in the old barrack-square, and the Adjutant used to drill us, and when he drilled us, he used to curse and swear. One day after he dismissed us, I went to him respectfully, with uncovered arms, and I told him that I was grieved to hear him utter such language out of his lips, and that it did no good to him, but corrupted others, and that God has said, " Thou shalt not take the name of the Lord thy God in vain ; for the Lord will not hold him guiltless that taketh his name in vain ; " and " Swear not at all." He seemed to be condemned in his conscience, and said he would try and not do it again. But he actually did it again, and I went the second time to him, and repeated the reproof in the same manner, and he turned very angry.

Some mornings the soldiers used to be an hour there before the parade began, and they met in groups of about a dozen in different places, talking about the battles they had fought, and the victories they had won. I was there as soon as they were, and I opened my mouth, and lifted up my voice like a trumpet, and showed them their sins. "Cry aloud, spare not, lift up thy voice like a trumpet, and show my people their transgression, and the house of Jacob their sins." (Isaiah lviii. 1.) I did that faithfully and fearlessly, and shut up all their refuges but one, and that was Jesus, who is " an hiding-place from the wind, and a covert from the tempest." The groups broke up, and came round about me, and heard me, and I made the square ring. One morning, to my astonishment, the Adjutant ordered me immediately to be confined in the black-hole, which is just above the arch as you enter the Castle. There is an iron plate now, to prevent the prisoners looking through, but there was none then. I could look through, and preach, and pray, and sing, and I gathered a great congregation below, who looked at me with astonishment. The commanding officer was coming by, and heard me, and ordered me immediately to be released. Next morning I was earlier in the barrack-square, and repeated preaching, and had a greater congregation than I had before, and they listened with greater attention. The Perth militia were in the Castle at that time, and their officers and non-commissioned officers, and privates came to hear me. Instead of the black-hole putting the fire out, it made it shine brighter. I had more courage, and was more bold the second time than the first. I say that to the glory of him that sent me to preach. The Adjutant, Gunn, on my preaching a second time, sent me away to the black-hole again. The men that used to persecute me, when they saw me put in the second time, said, "We will not persecute Robert any more; we see the root of the matter is in him." I was in the black-hole on a Sabbath day, and there were a number of thoughtless young men and young women that came into the Castle to hear the Perth band play, and I could see them through the stanchions of my window. My heart was in right tune, and I began to sing a sweet, melodious hymn or psalm, that arrested their attention, and astonished them. After I had done singing, I prayed a few words; telling the Lord their sin in breaking the Sabbath day, by coming to hear carnal music on carnal instruments. As far as I recollect, I prayed that the Lord might captivate their minds with heavenly music. Then I preached to them, and did not spare them. I studied to open their wounds before I applied the plaster.

The next day I was still in the same place, when the commanding officer, Major Rose, came into the

Castle, and the Lord gave me favour in his eyes. The parade fell in, and Major Rose ordered me to be released, and brought me out before the regiment and the Adjutant, and said to me, "Robert, what is the reason you have now been twice a prisoner in the blackhole?" I replied, "Please your honour, before the parade drum beat, the men of the regiment met in troops, and were telling the wars they were at, and the battles they had fought, and the victories they had won. I could have done the same, but I had better news to tell them. If they took liberty to tell news about the world and the wars, will you not give me liberty to tell good news from heaven?" "Yes, Robert, you have my liberty." This was before the Adjutant and the regiment. I asked the commanding officer if he would allow me to go through the barracks, to take the Bible with me, to read the Scriptures, and to pray. He said, "Robert, you have my leave, when duty does not interfere."

Another time, the chaplain of the Castle was in the barrack-square ; the officers encouraged me to speak to him, and I went. "You are the chaplain of the Castle, and especially of the 9th Veteran battalion. When we are formed into a square, occasionally you preach to us as if we were all Christians. If you knew the men as well as I do, you would warn them as did the prophet Ezekiel, who received the word from God, and God set him to be as a watchman to warn the house of Israel. Now, you have this regiment under your charge, and they are the worst men I ever knew. I can compare them to nothing but incarnate devils; it is by their fruits they are known. You should have lifted up your voice and cried aloud, and spared not, and shown them their sins, and the miserable life they lived, and that the end of such a life will be everlasting punishment. You should lead them to Christ, who died for sinners, and rose again, and is now 'exalted' as 'a prince and a Saviour, for to give repentance to Israel, and forgiveness of sins.' Now, when you do that, if the sinner dies in his iniquity, 'thou hast delivered thy soul;' but if you do not from God warn him, to save his life, 'the same wicked man shall die in his iniquity; but his blood will I require at thine hand.'" The commanding officer was present, and heard me speaking these words to the chaplain. He said, "Robert, what part of the Bible is that in?" I replied, "It is in two places; in the 3d chapter of Ezekiel, the 17th, 18th, and 19th verses, and in the 33d chapter, at the 7th, 8th, and 9th verses." "Robert," he said, "I will look at my Bible when I go home." Now, Mr Crawford, the chaplain, had not a word to say, and all the officers and men seemed to be well pleased, except the Adjutant. When I think of it now, I am astonished that I had such boldness and such liberty of speech, and warned them so faithfully. It was not I, but the Lord that commanded me to speak with authority, because he sent me, and I knew it. To his adorable, exalted name, be all the glory. I must

confess that, though I did all that he commanded
me, I should be an unprofitable servant; what I
did or suffered would not atone for one sin. I
rest entirely on the satisfaction and merits of the
Lord Jesus Christ; and I pray that he may wash
my person and services in his most precious blood,
and accept the same to the praise of his grace.
Glory be to the Father, Son, and Holy Ghost,
one God!

I was in the Castle at the time the three men
were executed on account of the New-year's-day
riot. I had then newly joined the 9th Veterans.
I got acquainted with the Quarter-master-serjeant
Shookledge, and his wife. We went on our knees
in prayer at the throne of grace, and earnestly
interceded for the three men at the time they were
on the scaffold. The bridge was drawn, and the
gates of the Castle were shut, and the guns were
manned to be ready in case of a riot, and not a
soldier was permitted to go out till all was over.
Blessed be the Lord, in his wise providence, he
brought good out of that evil; that was about
forty years ago, and there has never been a New-
year's-day riot like that since.

After being awakened and alarmed about my
sin, and misery, and danger, and after finding
peace with God, I made a conscience of having
family prayer twice a-day. In the Castle of Edinburgh I was obliged to be in the barracks, and I
still continued my practice there. I said to the
men in the barrack-room one morning, "Now I
am going to have worship; if any of you are in-

clined to join me, you are heartily welcome." I
began with singing, and reading the Word of God,
and prayer. As I was singing the hymn—

> " Lord, and am I still alive?
> Not in torments, not in hell;
> Still doth thy good spirit strive,
> With the chief of sinners dwell.
> Tell it unto sinners, tell,
> I am, I am out of hell!"

My back was towards the door, and I was standing on my feet, when a man came behind me.
I looked and saw that it was the gunner of the
Castle, who kept the canteen. All of a sudden he
struck me with his fist behind the right ear, and
knocked me down, and my head lighted on the
fender of the fire-place, which took my senses
away for a time. When I came to myself, I stood
up, and all the men of the barrack cried shame on
the gunner, and told me to go and report him.
"No," said I, "I will pray for him," and I continued the worship till it was over. I was informed a little time after that the man had no
peace in his mind; he went down to Newhaven,
when the tide was full, and drowned himself in the
sea. I thought of that passage, "Vengeance is
mine, I will repay, saith the Lord." But I still
persevered, notwithstanding all I met with.

There is one thing I must not omit to name.
When I came to the Castle, Dr Stewart lived in
George Square. He inquired for me, and, as I
did not happen to be in the barrack at the time,
he left his address for me to call on him that night,
and take tea with him. Carey's Baptist Mission

sent home periodical accounts from Calcutta concerning the work of our Lord in India, and he saw
my name there, in the 21st periodical account.    I
went that same night at the hour appointed, and
the late Dr, then Mr Innes, was there.    They used
to read, as I mentioned, the periodical accounts,
and that night I was a living witness, and a proof
of the success of Carey's Baptist Mission.    We
had a sweet conversation, and they were both
highly delighted to see one that came from Bengal, and who informed them what he saw, and
felt, and enjoyed.    Mr Innes invited me to his
church on the Lord's day and I went in my regimental clothes.    He introduced me to the church
when assembled, and said, "Here is a brother
come from Bengal, who was baptized by Mr Ward,
in the church at Calcutta;" and he requested me
to pray, and I was not backward to do so.    My
heart at the same time was full of grief for my old
sins that I had repented of, and full of my first
love to our Lord and Saviour Jesus Christ, because he forgave me, and washed me in his blood,
and gave me his spirit, to witness with my spirit
that I was a child of God.    All Edinburgh has
since that seen more than forty years' evidence of
this.    To him be all the praise, and to me the
shame and confusion of face.

When I was in the Castle, I was obliged to
sleep in the barrack, where the soldiers often
broke the laws both of God and man by intro-
ducing bad company.    I could not endure this
abomination, so one night, when the serjeant came

to put out the light after the roll-call, I told him
to do his duty. I knew that if he refused, and I
reported him, he should be brought to account.
The serjeant enforced the rule, and the men hated
me for what I had done. But I did not regard
their hatred; it was for me to do what my blessed
Lord commanded me, and not countenance sin.
He said, "They hated me without a cause," because he testified that their works were evil.

When I came to Edinburgh, I was inclined to
join Mr Anderson's church, which met then in
Richmond Court. Mr Anderson and all the
church seemed to be delighted with me for a while,
as I came from the Baptist church at Calcutta. I
thought the members were all perfect Christians.
They had a prayer-meeting once a week, and they
asked me to pray among them. In my prayers, I
generally showed the object of my prayer, God the
Father, seated on a throne of grace; the way of
access to him, through the incarnation of his Son,
and his active and passive obedience, and his
resurrection and ascension to glory; our need of
Christ's blood and righteousness, and of the aid of
the Eternal Spirit; and that through Christ we
have access by one Spirit unto the Father;" then,
making a hearty confession of our original and
actual sins, I pled earnestly for the forgiveness of
them all through the blood of the atonement.

About this time, the words that God spake
after he made man, came into my mind—"It is
not good for the man to be alone." I was a single
man, and was about thirty-five years of age. I

saw in the book of Proverbs, that "a prudent wife is from the Lord." I made prayer and supplication unto the Lord, that, if it was his will, he would direct me to one such as I have mentioned. I was to use the means, and the person whom the Lord appointed for me was to consent; and if I asked any that he had not appointed, she was to say no. There were no less than three that I spoke to, and they all refused, but the fourth consented. After I was married, she told me that she herself had prayed that, if it was the Lord's will that she should change her life, he would give her a praying husband or none at all. After we were a little while married, she burst into tears of joy, and said she had got her request; she had prayed for a praying husband, and had got one sent her all the way from the East Indies. I had thus the pleasure of having a praying wife, and we both gave thanks to the Lord for answering prayers. I thought that, being believers, if we acknowledged God in all our ways, he would direct our steps.

I had another object in marrying. Those men that were married had permission to live out of the Castle, in the town, away from the soldiers. I was sick of being among such characters, and was, like Lot, "vexed with the filthy conversation of the wicked," from day to day. We got a quiet house, where we could worship God without any to make us afraid. This was in the year 1813.

I still continued preaching in the Castle whenever I had opportunity, and the Adjutant could

not endure it. Such of the 9th Veterans as were
unmarried men, were to be sent to Shetland, and
he thought he would then get rid of me by sending
me there. He said, when the regiment was on parade, that the unmarried soldiers were to step out
of the ranks. When he saw me standing still
among the married, he said, " What, Flockhart, I
thought your religion did not permit you to marry!"
I replied (with emphasis) in that passage in Hebrews, 13th ch., 4th v. "Marriage is honourable
in all, and the bed undefiled : but whoremongers
and adulterers God will judge." When he heard
that, he was horror-stricken. Having a switch in
his hand, he struck his boot with it, and turning
on his heel, said, " I have been in many parts of
the world, and I never met with any one that
could beat me, till I met with Robert Flockhart,
and he would beat the very devil." All the men
burst out into laughter, and laughed at him most
heartily. Every time I mounted guard, men would
come—some to revile me, and some to ask me
questions, that they might have to accuse me, and
others would scoff at me. I saw the necessity of
having the wisdom of the serpent and the harm-
lessness of the dove, and I believe the Lord gave
it to me in a measure, because I prayed for it.
Sometimes also I had occasion, like David, to hold
my peace when the wicked were before me. One
time, in particular, my wife had brought my tea
to the guard-house. Before I took it, the corporal
of the guard was scoffing at me, and I thought I
would do as Paul did ; so I gave thanks in pre-

sence of them all. "And when he had thus spoken he took bread, and gave thanks to God in presence of them all : and when he had broken it, he began to eat." By what I said in that prayer, the Lord was pleased to touch his heart; for he afterwards told me that he went out of the guardhouse and wept sore. He became a converted man, and was instrumental in converting his wife. I was intimately acquainted with him in Edinburgh afterwards for many years. Up to the day of his death he always respected me, and was sorry for persecuting me. I often preached to the men when I was on the main-guard at night, and some wished that I were always on sentry, that I might not disturb them. I had rough work to do amongst them, but the Lord aroused me to deal faithfully with them, and made me lift up my voice like a trumpet, and cry aloud, and spare not. I set their sins in order before them, and showed them the miserable state they were in while they remained in them, and how they were in danger of that awful punishment threatened against such characters in the 9th Psalm, 17th v., "The wicked shall be turned into hell, and all the nations that forget God." Likewise in the 11th Psalm, 6th v., "Upon the wicked he shall rain snares, fire and brimstone, and an horrible tempest : this shall be the portion of their cup." When I saw that they were thoroughly awakened, I preached to them Christ crucified, and his resurrection from the dead, and his ascension to glory, and that he has sat down on the right hand of the

Majesty on high," and is now seated on his media-
torial throne, " a Prince and a Saviour, for to give
repentance to Israel and forgiveness of sins"—
that he is " the author and finisher of our faith."
I showed them that, to obtain this end, they must
use the appointed means ; by searching the Scriptures : " Search the Scriptures, for in them ye
think ye have eternal life ; and they are they
which testify of me ;" by earnest prayer, like the
publican and the prodigal son ; and by attending
to hear faithful sermons ; " Faith cometh by hearing, and hearing by the word of God." I saw
that I was in danger of being led away by my companions if I did not hold up the banner of the
Cross continually, but the Lord whom I served
gave me grace to declare his gospel, and who he
was ; he exercised me to be diligent " in season"
and " out of season," and by so doing I was kept
near to him, and preserved from being conformed
to them and their practices. I trust that, through
his blessing, my labours were not in vain.

There was in the Castle a little tower, to which
you went up by stairs. I often found that place
to be a Bethel to me, and I spent hours there by
myself in prayer and meditation, and reading the
Scriptures. I met with sore persecutions and
trials, but sought support and a blessing on my
labours, and that I might " be of good courage,"
which the Lord, in his condescending love,
granted.

I got liberty, when off duty, to work at my own
occupation as a smith. One shop where I wrought

was in the middle of the Nether Bow, down a stair. I used to reprove the workmen for swearing, and drinking, and bad conduct, and, while I told them what the consequences should be hereafter, I always pointed them to Jesus Christ. On Saturday, when we got our wages, they had a custom of going to the public-house to get change, and drink there. They were very anxious that I should go with them. But I refused ; and therefore they stopped a sixpence off my wages, and spent it in drink for themselves. It was against my will that they should drink with my money, but it was a rule with them. When I preached to my master, and he said he would kick me down stairs, I left him, and went to Mr Gilroy, who had a shop at the back of the Castle. I wrought with him a while, and there, as usual, I did not hide the light nor my colours. There was one man who was so mad at me, that he was frantic, and foamed at the mouth. He took up a shovel, and ran against me, and said he would knock my brains out. I did not shrink back, but held up my face to him. Unless the Lord had held his hand, I am sure he would have killed me. There was another man who wrought in the same stance with me, whose name was Mackellar, belonging to the 9th Veteran battalion. He was a great persecutor, and one day he got into a violent rage, and struck me on the cheek. To the astonishment of the bystanders, I turned round to him the other also, and this had more effect than if I had returned the blow, for I could have beaten him well, had not grace sustained and restrained me.

In this distressing state of matters, the Adjutant not liking to take me into the Castle, sent me away to do duty in Blackness Castle. This strong old fortress is built upon a rock that juts out into the Firth of Forth, about four miles north of Linlithgow. It is one of the gloomiest places any one could imagine, and contains a horrid dungeon, deep and dark like hell itself. Often did I think, when I looked down into this dreary pit, from which escape was impossible, how highly I was favoured in comparison with the host of noble Covenanters, among whom was the devoted Welsh, who were doomed to spend their lives here in languishing and sorrow. It was Welsh, who, in writing to one of his friends from this place, said, that " he was thankful to think that although he was in the darkness of blackness, he was not in the blackness of darkness." There was a party there of the 9th Veterans, under the charge of a godly officer. He was glad to see me there. This officer had two or three daughters, and he requested me to expound the Scriptures to them, which I did with great delight. When I came to the barracks, the men had got their monthly arrears, and were drinking. They saluted me when I went in amongst them, and asked, " What news from Edinburgh ?" I replied, " ' The wicked shall be turned into hell, and all the nations that forget God ; ' and those that get drunk are among the wicked that forget God." That kept them from flattering me, and kept me at a distance from their sins. There was a good man there that had a bed with curtains in the barracks. He kindly offered me his bed to accommodate me and my wife, agreeing to take mine; which offer I gratefully accepted. When I had worship night and morning, he would come, and creep away from the rest of the soldiers, and we three all joined together in the exercise. The wicked fellows in the barracks threw stones at me while I was engaged in prayer; but I still persevered, and that notwithstanding all opposition. I tried to reclaim them from their wicked courses, sometimes by kind counsels and encouragements from the word of God, telling them to flee to Christ, the only refuge from "the wrath to come." One night I was sitting at the fire, reading a sermon by Christopher Love on that text, "But rather fear him which is able to destroy both soul and body in hell" (Matth. x. 28). I read it out, that all in the barracks might hear, and it made one fellow get up in a rage. He struck me with his foot on the mouth, and brought blood from my lips. Another man, a great swearer, used to annoy me in the barracks. There was a cookhouse near them, to which I used to retire for prayer and meditation, and this swearer would try to prevent me from going in. I took him by the shoulder and wheeled him about, and gave him a good shaking; and when he found that I was too strong for him, he did not disturb me any more.

I spent as little time as possible in the barracks

during the day; and having got acquainted with a civilian and his wife, who had a private house in a village close by where we lay, I told them, as they were religious people, of my design to go through all the neighbourhood and preach the gospel. I got permission for my wife to remain with them during my absence, which they allowed with pleasure.

I went through Blackness town, and preached in various places there without opposition. After that I went to Linlithgow, and did the same thing. I persevered for about a month or six weeks, and through all the villages round about I saw that there was much need to arouse the people, for it was a dead and barren place. Mr Ryland says, " A minister is nothing worth who cannot make the devil roar." I had awakened by my preaching the magistrates in Linlithgow, and they sent a warning to the commanding officer in Blackness, that if the soldier came there again and preached, they would put him in the jail. The officer sent for me and showed me the letter, and told me the contents of it; but, being a godly man, he left it to my own will whether I would go again, or leave off. As he was so civil with me, I purposed in my mind that, to please him, I would not go again. I saw afterwards that that was wrong. I went out one day to take a walk by the sea-side, as I had plenty of time, my object being to meditate and pray. While travelling on, I came to a lane on my left hand, and a flock of birds flew over my head up the lane. They seemed to say, "Come up this way!" My fancy followed them, and I began to think, "Is there nothing in the Word of God that speaks about birds?" I remembered that passage—"But ask now the beasts, and they shall teach thee; and the fowls of the air, and they shall tell thee." They seemed to tell me that that lane led to Linlithgow. This gave me courage, so that I did not fear the threatenings of the magistrates; and I went boldly to the most public place, and began, as usual, first by singing, and then by prayer and preaching. I went afterwards to several places in the town. I was anxious that all should hear, my object being the conversion of their souls to God, through Jesus Christ, who opened up the way for them to come to God, and for God to come to them. I knew the value of their souls, and that the virtue and power of Christ's blood and righteousness is to remove the distance, and bring them nigh unto God by the blood of his cross. I hope that my labours in the Lord were not in vain. Though I do not see it now, it shall be seen at the day of judgment, that not a grain of the wheat has been lost. The magistrates of Linlithgow did not put me in jail. They threatened me, but I came away triumphantly, with a glad heart. A corporal was sent soon after to tell me to come back again to Edinburgh Castle, so I bade farewell to Blackness.

I come now to mention a very delicate dispensation of God's providence. Being connected with Mr Anderson's church, I one day told him that I had spoken to a soldier in the Castle about the concerns of his soul, the consequences that would await him at the day of judgment, and the necessity of applying without delay to Christ for grace to repent. He spoke very harshly to me, and said, "Who told you to preach? You must get the church's leave." I said—"When I see an opportunity to speak, must I come back to ask your leave and the church's first? I might lose the opportunity, and never see the person again." So he and I differed, and from that time I seemed to be a black sheep in his eyes. Some person sent him an anonymous letter. He blamed me for it, and although I had not written it, he put me under an arrest, not to sit at the Lord's table along with others. For several weeks I continued to ask him what I had done, that he should excommunicate me from the Lord's table. I wished to be told from his own mouth, but he would not tell me. One Sabbath day I came and sat at a distance from them that were at the table. After the services were all over they generally sat a short time, and my heart being full of grief for the treatment they gave me (they never would reason with me or give me a reason), I took this opportunity of unbosoming all my grief to the Lord audibly, before them all, and the most of them ran out of the church. I continued praying, however, until they stopped me by force. After that I came out and went home. I told my wife, and we both joined together in prayer and thanksgiving, and this brought great relief to my mind.

Next Sabbath day after that, I came from the parade in the Castle straight to the church, having on the soldier's gray coat. The man at the plate would not let me in ; and as I was forcing my way in, some of the members came and dragged me to the ground, and took me to the police-office in Park Place. They then went to the Castle, and lodged a complaint against me to the officers, and said I wanted to breed a disturbance in the church, which I did not. They sent a corporal and a file of guard to take me out of the police-office to the Castle, and they made me a prisoner in the guard-house, but the officer soon released me. However, they put my name up at the gate of the Castle, that I was not to go out on the Sabbath day, which was a sore grief to me. I went to a retired place in the Castle, and laid all my complaints before the Lord, and pleaded the promise—" Call upon me in the day of trouble, I will deliver thee, and thou shalt glorify me." At last the officer, seeing me quite peaceable, gave me favour in the eyes of the commanding officer, and he did not believe what was laid to my charge, and gave me my liberty.

I went to Mr Aikman's church for some time, and the gospel he preached healed my afflicted mind. Then I went to hear the Methodists in Nicolson Square. They were lively, especially in their prayers. I gathered they were not altogether sound in their doctrine. I may mention, that one Sabbath morning, before I withdrew from them, they had a prayer-meeting. I was present at seven o'clock, and the prayer leaders were not there in time, so the people that were there beckoned to me to begin. While I was engaged in prayer, one of their class leaders came in, and tried to stop me by giving out a verse of a hymn, and then he began to pray; but I was determined he should not put me down when I had begun, and my prayer was like Aaron's rod that swallowed up all the magicians' rods; he left off praying, and I continued. When I had done, he told me I had no right to pray there, and I replied, that if he had been there in time, I should not have begun first.

Then I went to hear Mr Grey (he was not Dr then) in the old Chapel of Ease belonging to the West Church parish. He was a man of burning zeal, and I longed for every Sabbath day that I might hear him. He took off his coat, and put on his pulpit cloak, and would sweat like the celebrated Whitfield, who said, "A pulpit sweat would heal the cold." He had a crowded congregation, who heard him very attentively. Mr Grey was removed from that place to one of the city churches.

Dr Gordon succeeded him in the Chapel, and I heard his first sermon. He did not read then. I continued with him, and began to like him, he was so clear and so scriptural in his doctrine. I went to his house to have a conversation with him, and said to him, among other things, that his doctrine nourished my soul. I told him that, although I was a Baptist, I would join with him.

He replied, that he loved the Baptists. Dr Stewart, whom I named before, was a Baptist, and, under God, Dr Gordon derived much benefit from intercourse with him. I continued with Dr Gordon till he died.

I now return to another subject which I mentioned before. When I was in barracks at the Castle, among wild men, I heard a voice from the Lord speaking to me in the same words he once spoke to Paul : "Be not afraid, but speak and hold not thy peace ; for I am with thee, and no man shall set on thee to hurt thee." I needed it, and without his aids I should never have stood, as will be seen by what I had to endure.

I reasoned with myself that the Grassmarket, which was the place where the martyrs had been put to death, was a proper place for my labours, because of the wicked characters in it, and their immorality, which was worse than that in the city of Calcutta. "While I was musing, the fire burned." So I went there, and lifted up my voice like a trumpet, and cried aloud, and spared not. I showed them their sin and their danger, and what a miserable thing it was to live in sin ; and "knowing the terror of the Lord" myself, I "warned them to flee from the wrath to come," and preached Christ and all his offices. I was very warm and very earnest. Who should come up and interrupt me but Dr Stewart. He felt my pulse, and looked at me. Having been in company with him before, I loved the man, and he prevailed on me to go with him, and I went.

He made me stand at the head of the West Port for a little, and he went up to my house, where my wife was, and informed her what he intended to do; but I was still ignorant of it. He came to me, and asked me if I would consent to go with a man to a fine country house, and remain for a few days. Having a great respect for Dr Stewart, and confidence in him as a Christian, I consented; and where did he send me, think you, but to Morningside Lunatic Asylum!

As soon as I got in, the governor, who was an Englishman, and had the charge of the whole place, shaved my head, and put a blister on it. I said to myself, "they have served me worse than they did Samson; they did not blister *his* head." I bore it patiently and submissively; and I had the same *daftness* when I preached in the streets of Edinburgh, on the day of the National Fast, April 25th, 1854, forty-one years after, as I had then. This happened in 1813, and it was a new thing for a man like me to preach in the street. I was like the man out of whom Jesus cast a legion of devils, who was found "clothed, and in his right mind," and who requested of Jesus that he might follow him. Jesus denied his request, and told him to go home to his friends, and tell them what great things the Lord had done for him. I did just the same. He went through the city of Decapolis, and I, likewise, went through the city of Edinburgh for forty-three years, preaching the gospel. Notwithstanding all the discouragements and opposition I met with,

I determined to do what the Lord had bid me, remembering his promise, "Thy shoes shall be iron and brass ; and as thy days, so shall thy strength be." I have realised in my experience the fulfilment of his faithful promise, and to his name be all the glory !

To return to Morningside. Sometimes I met with kind treatment ; but when I began to preach to the governor, he used to curse and swear at me. I laid the law before him, and then I preached the gospel. He got into a passion, and put me in confinement in a dark place, that they called the black-hole. I took all this in good part ; it made me the more earnest in prayer, first for him, and then for all the patients. He took me out after being there a while, and I was permitted to take a walk in the garden. They all went in to take their breakfast, leaving me in the garden. The place being unfinished, and the wall at one place not closed, and easy to get over, I deserted. I knew they would overtake me if I kept the straight road ; but as there was a plantation enclosed by a high wall, about three hundred yards from the gate, on the right hand side, I leaped over the wall, and hid myself amongst the trees until I thought they would be as far as my house and back again. Then I made towards home, and got to my house in safety, and fastened the door to let nobody in. But some person informed the parties that I was in my own house. They got a ladder, and looked in at the window, and saw me ; so I was delivered again into the hands of the

Philistines, to the grief of some of the neighbours, who cried when they saw me taken back again. On account of the promises the governor made me, I went with submission.

Dr Stewart sent a minister to see me, and he was a strange minister—he told me I should not read the Bible! I gave him a fright, so that he did not come again. "The Bible," said I to him, "is the only remedy God has provided to heal the afflicted mind, and to be my compass, to show me the road to him. Christ is the way, and the Bible reveals him in all his offices, names, and titles." He prevailed on the governor to take the Bible from me, and he did it. I assured him, if he took it away, I would eat no meat till I got it back again—if he starved my soul, he would starve my body too. And I kept my promise. He sent my meals regularly for three days, and I always sent them back again; so I fasted three days and three nights. He began to be alarmed lest I should die of hunger, and fell on a plan to prevent that. He brought a strong man with him, and laid me on my bed, and the strong man held my feet and my knees down, and he himself put his knee upon my breast. Having a large key in his hand, he thrust it into my mouth, and turned it so that my mouth was kept open, and he put in a spoonful of meat, and tried to make me swallow it. I thought, "One man may take a horse to the water, but twenty-four will not make him drink," so I coughed it up in his face and would not swallow it. When he saw he was beaten, he said, "I will give you the Bible." Said I, "Give me the Bible first." When it was brought, I offered up a short prayer that the Lord would bless his word to my soul; then I read a chapter before I would eat, and then I partook heartily.

The governor said he would take it from me again, but I said I would die before I would part with my Bible, so he let me keep it. Then he fell upon another plan, which was as bad as taking it away, for he confined me in my room, and shut the window-shutters, and left me in pitch darkness. When in the night time, about twelve o'clock, I heard the rain dashing on the window, I got up and broke the window-shutters, which were on the inside; but the stanchions remained. I found that I could not get out unless I got through without my clothes, so I put my clothes through the stanchions, and getting through myself, I then put on my clothes. I had tied two sheets together in a sailor's knot that would not slip, and having tied one end of the sheets to the stanchions, I lifted the window and out with the sheets and some of my clothes, and I went down like a sailor on a rope. It was two storeys high. Then away I ran, and scaled the walls, leaving the sheets as a signal that I was off, and I ran home to my own house, and got refreshment. My wife had left the outer door unbolted that night, and when I came to her own door and rapped gently, she said, "Is that you, Robert?" I said it was. She told me she was impressed in her mind that

I should come that night. I informed her what I intended to do. I knew, if I remained at home, they would be after me in the morning, so I purposed to go to my father's house in Old Kilpatrick.

But in place of taking the Glasgow road, I went to Queensferry. While I was waiting for the boat, I took off my clothes, and plunged into the sea, and began to swim, which I formerly delighted in, and I found great benefit from so doing ; it refreshed my body, and strengthened me for my journey. As soon as I got ready, I went on board, and on going across I spoke to the passengers and boatmen concerning the one thing needful. After landing, I spoke to the people at North Queensferry with great liberty, and in any place where I met with a human being. When I arrived at Dunfermline, I lifted up my voice in the High Street, and different other places of the town. I unfurled the banners of the Cross, and preached a free and full salvation through Christ. The people wanted to give me money, but my wife had given me a three-shilling piece before I left, and I would not take any from them. I preached to them without money and without price. When night came, it struck my mind that I would not take lodgings, as it would interrupt me in what I intended to do. I meant to spend the night season in prayer without disturbing any one, or being disturbed, so I went to a corn-field, and having a soldier's great-coat with me, wrapped up in a handkerchief, I unloosed it, and covered myself up with it, and lay down in the field all night. I spent the whole night almost in prayer and meditation, after the example of our blessed Lord. He often used to resort to the garden and other places in the open air, and spend there the whole night in prayer. When the morning came it rained a little, and I rose up to return back to my own house, and occupied the whole day in sowing the seed on my way home.

When I arrived at my own house, in Edinburgh, it being then dark, I entered without being observed by any one. My wife informed me that the police were employed to search for me. One wicked serjeant said, If I was out of hell, he would find me. Poor fellow! I said he would never see me there, and I hoped he would not be there himself, and I afterwards used means to reclaim him. Some time after, I saw him, and I invited him to my house, and entertained him kindly, and gently put him in mind of what he said, and I exhorted him and prayed for him.

The usage I got made me poorly in my health, and my wife nourished me, and gave me medicine and a week's rest. The police made search for me, and my wife kept the door always *snibbed* during that week. There was a closet high up above the door; it had a door to it, and was about six feet long, and about three feet broad; and my wife brought a table for me to get up into it every time there was a knock at the outer door. When the police came to see whether I was in the house, my wife told them to come in and search, that they might satisfy themselves.

When I got better, I went out openly to the Grassmarket and preached there again. The police apprehended me and took me to my own house, till they informed the governor of the asylum. He came, and brought a coach to take me back to Morningside. I refused to go unless he would let me keep my Bible, and leave the windows open where I was to be confined. He promised to do so for the future, and kept his promise; but every night, when I took my clothes off to go to bed, he took them away, and kept them till the morning.

The governor had a sister and a daughter there. His sister was very kind to me. His daughter, who was a very religious girl, said to me that, if I could convert her father, I should get the best chair in Heaven. I said, "I could not convert myself, much less your father; but I can use means, and ask the Lord to bless the means used for his conversion." That was all my object during the time I was under his charge. At length he was brought to a better state of mind, declaring that I was an inoffensive man. I think he had great confidence in me, for he asked me to shave him, and employed me to cut some of the patients' hair.

The governor used to make the servants take the patients out to walk in the garden, and he asked me to preach to them. I cannot recollect exactly what I said. There were two or three

ministers in the asylum then, and what I did say
put two of them in a rage, and they cursed me.
What Ryland says, as mentioned before, was verified in the case alluded to.

I was kept nearly six months in that place—
from the 27th May to the 14th November 1814.
During that time the Lord taught me many sweet
lessons experimentally; it was a college for me.
My prayers were earnest, and fervent, and impor-
tunate from a broken heart, on account of the
afflictions of my confinement, and the accusation
that I was "beside" myself. It was the same with
my blessed Lord and Master; he always prayed
earnestly, but when he was "in agony, he prayed
more earnestly" that the cup might pass from
him, and then he qualified it with a "nevertheless
not my will, but thine, be done."

I got paper, pen, and ink, and wrote a few lines
to Dr Stewart, and got my letter conveyed to him
by my wife, who came to see me. Dr Stewart
got me out on the condition that I was not to
preach again. I thought whether I would obey
God or man. As I said before, God made me
speak, and not hold my peace; I was like a man
delivered, as David was, from the lowest hell;
and I dared not do otherwise.

There was another thing very remarkable while
I was in Morningside. There was a gentleman in
the asylum who was sensible at times; but often
trouble of mind came upon him, and he would
rage, and curse God, and curse his Son, and even
curse the blood of Christ. I went to visit him,

and went down on my knees beside him, with the Bible open before me. I pleaded what the Lord Jesus had done before, praying earnestly that he would do the same to this man, so that he might return to his right mind, and that the evil spirit might be cast out of him. But I observed it had no effect.

There was a fine young lady there, and she was in a deplorable state of mind. She longed for death. She would hold out her arms wide open, and clasp her hands, and say, "How I would embrace death!" I spoke to her, and said everything I could say to give her comfort. I asked her, Had she done anything in her life that had unhinged her mind; she replied, "No;" but refused to be comforted, notwithstanding all I told her. The servants used to take the patients to walk in the garden, and one day the young lady took her shawl, and tied it to a tree by one end, and put the other round her neck. The servants, observing her, screamed out, and the servant-men heard, and came and took her down. She was not dead outright, but recovered. However, the second time she finished herself, and obtained what she so much longed for. They kept it a secret; but the servants told me she hanged herself until she was quite dead.

There is another thing I wish to relate. While I was in the asylum, when alone in my room, I prayed to the Lord that he would lead me by his word and spirit into the "imagery" of my heart, and make his word to be "a discerner of the thoughts and intents" of my heart, and make me to know my sins that I had committed against him. I thought upon all my ways and actions through the whole course of my life, from a child to the present time. I confessed them over the head of my New Testament scape-goat, even Jesus Christ typified by that goat which Aaron was to present "alive before the Lord, to make an atonement with him, and to let him go for a scape-goat into the wilderness."

Having set all my sins before me in battle array, being full of grief on account of my old sins and offences against such a kind, loving, patient, and long-suffering Jehovah, I preached to myself as I would to a congregation. "Knowing the terror of the Lord," I threatened myself with the law: "Cursed is every one that continueth not in all things which are written in the book of the law to do them;" and "When the commandment came, sin revived, and I died." Then I went to the garden, where our Lord Jesus was "in an agony," and from thence to Calvary; and then I gave myself encouragement from that text, "For what the law could not do, in that it was weak through the flesh, God sending his own son in the likeness of sinful flesh, and for sin condemned sin in the flesh;" and "Whom God hath set forth to be a propitiation through faith in his blood, to declare his righteousness for the remission of sins that are past, through the forbearance of God; to declare, I say, at this time his righteousness; that he might be just, and the justifier of him which believeth in Jesus" (Rom. iii. 25, 26). This is only a specimen of what I did and said. I then concluded with prayer, with mine eyes looking up to Christ in faith, as the children of Israel that were bitten looked at the brazen serpent, and I found it was the only remedy for the mortification of my indwelling sin.

The sending me to Morningside was beneficial to me in an unexpected way. When the 9th Veteran battalion was to be broken up, the men had to go to Chelsea to pass the Board, and they got pensions according to their servitude. I, being in Morningside, had not to go up. My time of service being only twenty-one years and a half, it would have entitled me to no more than one shilling a day. Major Rose, whom I have before mentioned, wrote a letter about me to the Board, and getting the information that I was in Morningside Lunatic Asylum, they put me down deranged, and gave me a pension of one shilling and three-pence a day, which I have received now for nearly forty-two years. What an advantage it is to be religious! "All things work together for good to them that love God, to them who are the called according to his purpose."

I wish to relate here what I omitted before. While in Morningside, I at one time felt such a clear sense of God's favour, and of his reconciled countenance shining upon me in the face of Jesus Christ, that I said in my heart, like David, "I shall never be moved. Lord, by thy favour thou hast made my mountain to stand strong." But afterwards the Lord hid his face from me, and he permitted the angry powers of hell to set on me such strong temptations and evil suggestions as these :—"You are here in the madhouse, and all the world is against you, even the people of the Lord, for they put you here. Think of the unkind usage you are still receiving at their hands." Satan and his angels hurled their fiery darts against my soul to destroy me. Well, I was walking one day in the garden, and finding a piece of cord, I picked it up, and took it to my room. As soon as I got there, Satan tempted me to put the cord round my neck and hang myself, and I should undoubt-edly have obeyed his suggestion if God had not interfered. I could then say like Job, "My soul chooseth strangling, and death rather than my life." The devil would have triumphed if I had been left any longer to myself; but in his love and mercy God gave me, as it were, a *blink* of his re-conciled countenance, and in my heart I heard a voice saying, "Do thyself no harm!" No one knew of this fiery conflict but myself, and although I am very loth to let my weakness be known to my fellow men, yet my desire to be useful to those that may be so tempted, and also my desire to tell the truth in all things, have caused me to let the circumstance be known.

So the Lord brought me off again with flying colours, and I returned once more to my own house. When I got home, I was determined to give myself up entirely to the Lord's service, and begin again my old work of preaching the Gospel,

in which I took great delight.   The feeling of my
heart was, that the Lord should use me in any
way he thought best for his own glory.   I had a
stout body, a good constitution, and a willing
mind, and I was willing, and indeed very anxious,
to devote them all to the glory of God.   I constantly prayed that I might be made useful in the
Lord's work.

I determined to begin a school.   I began with
only *two* scholars, but one told another that I had
taken up a school, and it is surprising how soon
it spread.   In a short time I had *fifty* scholars.

The reason of my opening a school was this.
The wife of the drum-major of the regiment in
which I was serving had a boy who had never
been at school.   I heard of it, and offered to take
him under my care, and teach him.   My offer
was accepted.   The boy came, and I began to
teach the letters.   At this period of my history,
I was still in a state of nature.   Nevertheless I
was anxious to make myself useful.   So I entered
heartily into the work, and my pupil got on so
well, that in a short time he was as good a
scholar as myself, and before I left the regiment
I had the satisfaction of seeing him employed in
marking the various articles belonging to the men
who lived in the room with him.   And to show
the advantage of trying to do good, I may mention
that, whilst teaching this boy, I never drank like
the other men, as I wished to set a good example
before him.

In commencing a school after my conversion,

my object was not so much to make the children good scholars, as good Christians. I thought it would be a beautiful thing to get the Word of God instilled into their hearts. I commenced every morning with singing and prayer, and concluded with the same. This course I regularly pursued all the time I taught in Lauriston, which was twenty-five years, and I trust that my labours have "not been in vain in the Lord." During that time many died who belonged to my school, and, I trust, not a few of them "died in the Lord;" for some of them, who had ungodly fathers and mothers, astonished their parents by saying, in their dying moments, "They were going to be with Jesus in heaven." One of my scholars became a minister; another became a missionary, and was sent out to Africa.

When a boy I attended the school of Joseph Robertson in Edinburgh. His practice was to make his scholars commit to memory portions of the Scriptures and the Shorter Catechism with proofs, and afterwards repeat them to him. I resolved to follow the same plan in my school, having derived so much benefit from it myself.

One passage, which I learned at that school, was Isaiah i. 18.—" Come now, and let us reason together, saith the Lord : Though your sins be as scarlet, they shall be white as snow; though they be red like crimson, they shall be as wool." This text the Lord hid in my heart for fully twenty years. During all that time I had clean forgotten it. At length the Lord was pleased to

afflict me, and bring me into the wilderness that
he might draw me to himself, as it is written, " I
have loved thee with an everlasting love, therefore
with loving-kindness have I drawn thee." The
Spirit of God strove with me through the once
crucified but now glorified Saviour to lead me to
pray. I said I do not know how to pray, or what
to say. Then it came into my mind that I could
offer the Lord's prayer. Then, methought, I felt
not satisfied with praying the Lord's prayer only.
And now that the task learned so long ago at Mr
Robertson's school came into my mind, " Come
now, and let us reason together, saith the Lord,"
etc., etc., I repeated that blessed portion of God's
Word, and the Lord came to me, and I came to
him, and pleaded the fulfilment of that sweet
promise. I now understood why the Lord required me to confess my sins and transgressions,
—it was that his justice might be glorified in my
eternal punishment for breaking his law, and
living a life of rebellion against him. When,
therefore, I repeated the words, " Though my
sins be as scarlet, they shall be white as snow ;
though they be red like crimson, they shall be as
wool," I had the full assurance of faith that God
had heard and answered this my first prayer.
Thus, judging from my own case, I thought that
portions of God's Word, instilled into the children's
young hearts, might afterwards be productive of
great good, though I might not live to see it. It
might, I thought, be twenty or even thirty years
before the seed sown would ripen into fruit. No

matter; the attempt ought to be made, and the result left with God. The attempt, therefore, I did make, praying at the same time that, as in my own case, the fruit of my labours might appear (even though it should be many years hence) in the lives of at least some of my pupils.

I might say much more about my attempts to do good to the children entrusted to my charge, but I forbear. I now began to wish for more extensive usefulness, so I prayed unto the Lord that he would open up to me another field of labour. I thought that, as I had access to the young, I might also have access to the afflicted in the Infirmary, and God was pleased to open up the way for me.

About this time, an Englishwoman, on her way from Edinburgh to Glasgow, was overtaken by some ruffians, who abused her, and then left her half dead on the roadside. She was brought to the Infirmary, and her distressing case excited a deep sympathy and interest amongst the religious ladies of Edinburgh, many of whom came to see her, and to converse with her on the concerns of her soul. I was requested to go and see her, and pray for her. Not satisfied with visiting one unfortunate fellow-creature, I proceeded to visit and pray with all the other patients in the ward, and experienced great liberty and delight in doing so. I have been thus particular in describing the way in which I was led first to the Infirmary, because it was the commencement of a pleasant work, which continued for twenty years

I shall now proceed to mention some of the most interesting cases that came under my notice. I may observe at the outset, that having been, whilst I was a soldier in India, so long the inmate of an hospital myself, I felt a deep interest in all the patients I visited. Having been afflicted myself, I could sympathize with them in their afflictions. Besides I owed (under God) whatever spiritual peace or comfort I enjoyed to my having been an inmate of an hospital; for it was there, through the means of a religious comrade, who came to pray with me, that my heart was melted, and a praying spirit was produced.

The patients, I may observe, were all glad to see me when I visited them, and used to invite me back again. I took a pleasure in my work, and was encouraged in it by many passages in the Scriptures; for example,—"I was sick, and ye visited me" (Matt. xxv. 36); "The prayer of faith shall save the sick, and the Lord shall raise him up" (James v. 15); "The effectual, fervent prayer of a righteous man availeth much" (James v. 16). I have seen many instances in which these promises were fulfilled. I saw many deaths in the hospital, and the sight had, I trust, a salutary effect, in the way of quickening my zeal to save souls, and stirring me up to increased diligence and activity to make my "calling and election sure." Some of the patients would say, when they sent for me, that their ministers refused to come to see them for fear of the fever. I feel some delicacy in making these statements;

however, I wish to be honest, and to tell the truth. The patients used to say, " Mr Flockhart is not afraid of the fever." And they said the truth. I was not afraid, and never caught the infection during the twenty years I came to the hospital. Not so with the doctors, for many of them caught fever and died. I must at the same time state, that I never rashly and unnecessarily exposed myself, but endeavoured, while speaking to them, and praying for them, to keep at such a distance as not to inhale their breath, and took care also not to swallow my spittle.

I shall now proceed to give some instances of answers which were graciously accorded to my prayers whilst a visitor in the Infirmary.

A woman in one of the wards was apparently dying. Her limbs were contracted, her speech gone, her eyes were glazed, and the death-rattle was in her throat, as I thought. I was standing by her bedside. She observed me, and by her looks seemed to say to me, " Pity me, and pray for me ! " I did pray for her, in the name of Christ, with heart and soul, and went away, never expecting to see her again in this world. I came back to the same ward the week after. To my astonishment, I saw her sitting up in her bed ! I again spoke to her and prayed with her, thanking the Lord in my prayer from bringing her up from the gates of death, and took my leave. At the end of another week I returned, and found her sitting at the fireside with some of the other patients. I again spoke to her, and improved

her case to them all, to the best of my power.
At the end of the third week, I found her walking
through the hospital. Shortly after, she was dismissed, cured, from the Infirmary. I related the
circumstance to some godly people whom I
happened to meet at tea, one evening some time
after the occurrence took place, and there happened to be a young lady present who knew the
woman whose remarkable recovery I have described, and stated that she had heard the same
story from her own lips. I never saw or heard
of her afterwards, and am therefore unable to say
whether her soul was converted or not. I can
only state that I heard a favourable report of her
conduct from the young lady already referred to,
who was a Sabbath school teacher.

During my intercourse with the patients in the
Infirmary, I believe I saw hundreds die ; but most
lamentable to think, out of the whole number
(judging from appearances), only *one*, and he a
young man, the son of a godly father, " died in
the Lord." His last words to his father, who
was at his bedside during the last struggle, were,
" I know that I am going to glory ! " The others
seemed to " take a leap in the dark," not knowing
whether they were going to heaven or hell. If
we may institute a comparison between the ocean
of time and the ocean of eternity, then I think we
may compare the escape of the mariners and passengers who were shipwrecked with Paul, to the
death of believers. I would be inclined to compare the death of this young man who died in the

full assurance of faith, to the escape of the mariners of Paul's company who *swam* to land. It is my wish, however, to be charitable, and to judge charitably of all men, in all cases where that is possible. If we were to judge of the fate of our fellow-men hereafter, merely by their state of mind at death, I believe we should often find ourselves mistaken. Even our Lord himself was under a cloud for a time, before his death. This is evident from his sending forth the awful and heart-rending cry, "My God, my God, why hast thou forsaken me!"

.    .    .    .

But I go on to observe, that I never attempted faithfully to perform any duty to God, or to the souls of my fellow-men, without always encountering opposition, scoffs, and persecution. However, like Moses, "I esteemed the reproach of Christ greater riches than the treasures in Egypt," for I "had respect unto the recompense of the reward," not as a debt for what I did and suffered, but as the free gift of God. I knew that grace would reward what grace had done.

I have often said that the Christian life is a continual warfare, and all who live godly shall suffer persecution. The truth of this was often experienced by me, whilst visiting in the Infirmary. I suffered persecution both from the doctors and students. The patients, however, loved to see me. I may mention the names of two of the former in particular. The first was Surgeon ——, said to be a son of King William, the Fourth, or of the Duke of Kent. He was a clever, good-looking young gentleman. He was seized with illness, and Principal Baird, as the King's chaplain, requested to be admitted to visit him and pray with him. His reply to the Principal was, that he "wanted a physician, not a parson." He recovered, saw me in his ward one day, and took a dislike to me. There was at that time a good man lying ill in the ward, under the care of this young gentleman. He used to say, when he saw me, "Here is Mr Flockhart coming: he is a good man, and brings us good tidings." Such expressions of kindness and goodwill attached me to that ward ever afterwards.

One day I happened to be on my knees engaged in prayer, when one of the surgeons sent his clerk to tell me to cease, and come and speak to him. I persevered, however, and cried to God to send an arrow into the hearts of his enemies, and bring them down under him. He waited until I had done praying, and then came forward and asked me what was the reason I did not come to him when he sent for me. I replied that I was busy speaking to the Lord in prayer for myself and the patients ; but now that my prayer was over, I would, as it was my duty, hear what he had to say with all due respect. He said in reply, that he would tell the gate-keeper of the Infirmary not to let me in again. I spoke to the gatekeeper on the subject, and told him what Surgeon J—— had said. But he informed me, for my comfort, that he would receive no orders from any of the doctors, but only from the managers. I carefully studied to avoid giving offence either to Jew or Greek in the church of God on all occasions, but still, notwithstanding, I did not escape persecution.

I suffered persecution from another medical man, Surgeon O——. One time I happened to be engaged in prayer, with my hat by my side, when this gentleman came in, and, thrusting his stick into my hat, attempted to place it on my head. I shook it off my head, and still continued praying. On this he ran out of the ward until I was done. He then came in upon me like a lion, and said, "If I see you here again, I will tar and feather you." I replied, "I wonder a minister's son would say the like of that." He did not carry his threat into execution, however, and I studied afterwards to come to his ward when he was at dinner.

One day, whilst I was engaged at my usual work in the Infirmary, a number of the students came about me, and laying hold of me, attempted to drag me out of the ward. I laid hold of the iron bedstead, and held on by it until they pulled it along with me. So they were beaten in their attempt, and left me. I continued to persevere, notwithstanding all the opposition I experienced. I knew that the Lord was with me, and made my efforts to benefit the souls of my fellow-men successful. Hence the opposition of the powers of darkness.

I sometimes used to preach for Mr Porteous in

a room in the Infirmary set apart for that purpose.
On these occasions all the patients who were able,
were invited to attend.

One day a Popish priest came to administer
"extreme unction" to a young woman who was
apparently dying of fever. Going up to the bedside, he began to mutter, in a low tone of voice,
but with great rapidity, some words in Latin. I
happened to be present at the time, and seeing
what was going on, went down upon my knees,
and when the priest began to pray in Latin, I
began to pray to the Lord in English—not like
the priest in an unknown tongue, but in a language which they could all understand. In my
prayer I *levelled at the priest*, and prayed that
the Lord would have mercy upon those who
suffered themselves to be deluded by Popish
superstitions, and who put their trust in man
instead of God. My prayer made him tremble.
He became quite scared, and went up to the
nurse and asked her to make me hold my peace.
The nurse replied that she dared not, for I had
permission to come there when I pleased. I
persevered in prayer until he ran out of the
ward. I think I then went to the young woman
when the priest took his departure, and told her
to apply to the Lord Jesus Christ by prayer, and
he would send the Holy Spirit to anoint her soul
with the unction which cometh from above, and
to work in her repentance towards God, and faith
towards the Lord Jesus Christ.

I now proceed to mention another case. A

young woman was brought into the hospital in a very distressing state of mind, as well as of body. She grew worse as she approached her end, and alarmed all the patients and nurses in the ward with her, by her cries and lamentations. She said she felt as if there was fire in her bosom, and she tried to put it out by drinking large quantities of cold water. The nurse who attended her told me that she drank a whole stoup of water, which came up again as fast as she drank it. She had, it appears, given birth to an illegitimate child, and this was the cause of the anguish and remorse she exhibited on her death-bed. May her untimely and most distressing end prove a beacon and a warning to others. When tempted to transgress the laws of God and of their country, let them remember the fate of this unfortunate young woman.

Another case, very similar to that just described, came under my notice during my visits to the hospital, which I shall here relate as an additional warning to young women in service. In a respectable family in Edinburgh, where a number of servants were kept, one of the domestics attempted to commit suicide by cutting her throat. Fortunately she was discovered before life was extinct, and immediately conveyed to the Infirmary. The doctors staunched the bleeding, stitched up the wound, and to enable her to breathe and speak, put a silver tube into her throat. During the time she was under medical treatment in the hospital, I often visited her for the purpose not only of administering spiritual consolation, but also of leading her to form a just estimate of her sin against God and against her own soul. The particulars of her case were as follows :—She had an illegitimate child to a black-smith, and to hide her disgrace, had murdered her infant, and concealed it afterwards in her chest. Her fellow-servants told her master their suspicions —search was made in consequence, her trunk was opened, and the dead body of the infant was found in it. On this discovery the unfortunate woman cut her throat, and, as before narrated, in this condition brought to the hospital, where I saw her and learned her history. As soon as she was fit to be removed from the Infirmary, the blacksmith took lodgings for her, whither I followed her, being deeply concerned for her salvation. I told her she had been guilty of two crimes—the *murder* of her *child*, and the attempted murder of her own *soul* as well as of her *body;* for had she died in the condition in which she was discovered, she must inevitably have been lost for ever.

There was another case very like the two pre-ceding ones. A woman who lived in the West Port had a child, and murdered it, after which she buried it beneath a heap of stones behind the Castle. After this she went almost distracted, and in this awful state of mind went to the police-office at the head of the West Port, and delivered herself up. The police brought her to the Infir-mary, placed her in the *iron Ward,* put a straight waistcoat upon her, and tied her feet to an iron bed. I went to see her, and used all scriptural means to drive despair from her mind. I prayed for her, and in my prayer I pleaded the command, "put me in remembrance," etc. (Isaiah xliii. 26). I put the Lord in remembrance of his prayer for his murderers, "Father, forgive them, for they know not what they do" (Luke xxiii. 34). I am sorry to say that I had no evidence of any saving change being produced on the mind of this unhappy woman by my prayers and exhortations. She told me *that the child seemed constantly to stand before her eyes.* And in this most miserable condition she died.

Whilst I visited the Infirmary I saw many sights which it would be imprudent in me to describe, or even to allude to. The cases I have mentioned, however, furnish a specimen of them.

I used to visit the Lock Hospital, and from what I there saw and heard, I was led to entertain more hope of the conversion of the harlots than of many of the characters of which I have been speaking. My prayers and admonitions used often to draw tears from the eyes of these unfortunate creatures. On my departure they used to follow me to the door, and implore my assistance and aid to deliver them from their sinful and miserable way of life. My answer was, "Apply to Mr Porteous for admission into the Magdalene Asylum." I went to the Lock Hospital of my own accord, out of love to Christ and to save souls. Having myself first been brought to a knowledge of the truth in an hospital, I thought it my imperative duty to strive to do for others in my own country what God had done for me in a foreign land. I therefore preached the Gospel during the day, and prayed for a blessing upon it during the night. Whilst labouring to water others, the Lord was pleased to water my own soul, and thus my employment became my profit as well as my delight. I hope and trust that it will be seen in the judgment-day that my labours have not been in vain in the Lord.

I used to visit the Canongate Jail at times for Mr Porteous ; likewise Bridewell on the Sabbath day, as well as the Trades' Maiden Hospital, and several other public institutions.

I now come to another part of my history as a street-preacher in Edinburgh, which I neglected to state at the proper place. The reader of these pages will remember that I commenced my career as a public speaker in the Castle. One day, whilst on the main-guard, during the period I lay in the Castle, one of the soldiers was cursing and swearing, and I was reproving him for it, and showing him the evil consequences of the course he was pursuing, and was getting warm on the subject, when who should come up at the moment but the senior lieutenant-colonel, and he spoke in a voice of authority to the officer of the guard, saying, " I order that man (meaning me) to be relieved of guard, and to do no more duty." This was indeed joyful news to me, so I immediately took off my accoutrements and went home.

# PART IV.—THE STREET PREACHER

I NOW began to preach through the streets of
Edinburgh. Wherever I saw a man committing
sin, I reproved him, and then a multitude would
gather round me. I would then begin to speak
to them from a text of Scripture, and would continue to speak so long as there was any one to
hear. Then the policemen would lay hold of me,
and drag me off to the police-office, and my wife
would get me out, and I would begin to preach
again, as if nothing had happened. I remember
preaching in Buccleuch Street, in Lauriston,
where I lived, also in the West Port and in the
Grassmarket.

I was four times put in the police-office in the
West Port for preaching the Gospel, once in Hope
Park, then again for preaching in the Castle Hill
and High Street. Altogether, I was nine or ten
times in prison for preaching the Gospel in Edinburgh. Captain Brown, the superintendent of
police, had been an officer in the 79th regiment.
It was said that his lady was an Irishwoman, and
she prevailed on her husband to have chiefly Irish
policemen, who were very severe upon me, as
they could not bear my preaching, which was not
intended to please men. I remembered that the
Lord commanded Jonah to "preach the preach-

ing " that he " bid " him, and I knew if I preached another " preaching," I was not the Lord's servant. One day, when I was in prison for preaching the Gospel, Captain Brown came in and said, " Where is that preacher ? " I immediately answered, " Here." " Stand up," said he, " that I may hear you preach." I obeyed his command, and what I said to him on the occasion made him a little like Felix. " Oh," said he, " I see you can preach ; come down." I always saw it to be my duty to preach to the policemen, in whatever police-office I might be in. I said to myself,. these men cannot get to church, and who knows but the Lord has sent me to preach to them, and I will preach to them. I never saw the police-office yet where the inmates were anxious to keep me long a prisoner ; they were always too glad to get me out.

I also preached for some time on the Calton Hill on Sabbath nights, and likewise in the King's Park. One day I happened to be at the foot of Niddry Street, and saw two women decoying some soldiers into their den. So I lifted up my voice and cried aloud, " Beware, soldiers, beware! If you go into their house, remember it is the way to hell, going down to the chambers of death." The noise I made alarmed the whole neighbourhood ; the women fled into their house, and the soldiers ran away, being ashamed. Having now a large congregation around me, I began to preach, and continued preaching until a man came up and threw a bucket of water upon me. It appears that this man was a dyer, and lived at the foot of Niddry Street. His wife happened to be looking out of her window when I was addressing the soldiers and the bad women, and thinking herself included with the latter, she got her husband to give the aforesaid salutation to cool me. This did not cool my ardour, nor drown my love for perishing souls. On the contrary, it made the fire of my zeal burn brighter and clearer, and caused the people to pay more attention to what I said.

There happened to be present on the occasion a man named Campbell, a shoemaker, who was very much given to drink. My words apparently were blessed to him, as I afterwards ascertained from himself. I asked him what the particular expression was which produced the salutary change. He replied that it was contained in Deut. xxxii. 29—"Oh that they were wise; that they understood this, that they would consider their latter end!" That counsel Moses gave to the children of Israel before he was taken from them. I kept an eye upon this man after that, as long as he lived, and I saw nothing in his moral conduct inconsistent with his Christian profession. He died, so far as I could judge, in the faith.

After this, I felt an earnest desire to see the prisoners in the jail, especially those who were under sentence of death. My wish was gratified, and I was admitted into the prison.

There was at that time one MacIntyre lying in

the jail under sentence of death. It appears he
had been concerned in an attempt at housebreaking in the Lothian Road, near Isaac Scott's.
The policeman on duty, being at his post, de-
tected the thieves. They took to flight; he
pursued, and caught MacIntyre in the West
Church Poor-house green. On being apprehended,
he refused to disclose the names of his accomplices, saying he would " *hang first.*" The men
that were with him were taken soon after, and
committed to prison. On their examination they
denied the crime with which they stood charged;
and as there were none to bear witness against
them, they were set at liberty. In due time
MacIntyre's trial came on, and he was found
guilty of attempting housebreaking and robbery,
and was sentenced to die. I learned from him
that his father was an Irishman, and his mother
a Scotchwoman, and a Protestant. His mother,
he said, taught him many portions of God's Word,
and he was not ignorant of the Bible. He
formerly resided in Glasgow, where, I understand
he was much respected by his friends and acquaintances. Being a member of the Glasgow
Highland Society, an effort was made by in-
fluential individuals connected with that institution, to obtain his pardon, but in vain. I was
with him the day before he left the jail to go to
the Lock-up. Poor fellow! I won his confidence,
and he told me the state of his mind, which he
would not do to one of the city clergy, a man of
cold and distant manners. He said that if he

obtained a pardon, he had made up his mind to
preach to the convicts when he was in banishment. At this moment the clergyman came into
the cell, and the prisoner asked him if he had any
good news for him? He answered "No;" and
putting his hand into his pocket, pulled out a
letter which informed the unhappy man that his
petition would not be forwarded to the sovereign.
On this the prisoner became deeply affected. Dr
—— then withdrew, telling me that I was to
speak to him, and pray with and for him.

As soon as Dr —— was gone, I told the
prisoner that there was no mercy for him from
man; that every door was shut against him but
one, and that door was Christ. I told him that
Jesus would not refuse to receive him; that he
was the way, as well as the door, and that whosoever came to him, he "would in nowise cast
out." I told him, moreover, that by "his incarnation, obedience, and death, he had finished
transgression, made an end of sin, and brought in
an everlasting righteousness." Then he went to
prayer, and if ever a man was earnest for the
salvation of his soul, and appeared ready to meet
his God at that moment, it was that man. On
rising from our knees, he was very anxious that
we should sing something. I asked him what we
should sing; he replied—

"The hour of my departure's come."

While singing it, I glanced at his countenance,
and his very soul seemed to be wholly engaged

in worship, so earnest and devout was his appearance. After singing the hymn, Mr Porteous, the chaplain of the jail, brought in four men who had been apprehended on suspicion, that MacIntyre might say a few parting words to them, which he did in the most earnest and impressive manner. In his address, he urged them to "flee from the wrath to come," to seek repentance and the remission of their sins from Jesus Christ, who is exalted to bestow these blessings upon all who sincerely and earnestly ask them. He also spoke to them of the necessity of praying for the Holy Spirit, whose office it was to convince of sin, and to make the sinner feel his miserable condition whilst he continued in sin. Another reason, he said, why they should pray for the Holy Spirit was, because in the reading of the Scriptures, he enlightened the mind in the knowledge of Christ and him crucified, and renewed the will, and enabled us to embrace the Saviour as our prophet, priest, and king.

To all he said, these four men paid the greatest attention, because, as it seemed to me, their lives were, in a great measure, in his hand. Had he informed upon them, as it is probable he could, their lives would have been forfeited to the violated laws of their country. In consequence, however, perhaps of the hasty expression, "I'll hang first," to which he had given utterance when first apprehended, when asked to give the names of his partners in the attempted robbery, he still held out, and refused to give the authorities the desired information.

Thus we see how faithful worldly men are to one another. And surely their conduct in this respect should furnish a lesson to Christians. If worldly and wicked men can be faithful to their associates in sin, surely Christians should be faithful to God and to each other. Here is a man who may be said to have laid down his life for his wicked companions. Had he turned "king's evidence," he would no doubt have obtained his liberty. But he remained true to his word, and sacrificed his own life to save theirs! How much more ought believers to lay down their lives for their brethren.

I shall now give the particulars of another remarkable case that came under my notice. It was that of a man named Gilchrist, a native of Edinburgh, and in comfortable circumstances. He was connected with a company who ran stage-coaches between Edinburgh and Glasgow. Hearing that a large sum of money was to be forwarded from a Glasgow bank to Edinburgh by one of his coaches, he disguised himself in a woman's dress, got instruments for breaking open the chest containing the treasure, and secured a suitable seat in the coach. When he had robbed the coach, he left it at the nearest stage, and put on his usual dress. But his brother and he, being suspected, were in a short time apprehended, and, by circumstantial evidence, one of them was ultimately condemned to death.

When the prisoner found himself shut up in the condemned cell, he grew distracted at the thought of being made a public example, and became very unmanageable. Mr Rose, the governor of the jail, thought it expedient to get some godly man to read the Scriptures to him, and endeavour to compose his troubled mind. He sent for me, and I went at his request. I found the prisoner in a most agitated and anxious state of mind, eagerly wishing that his life should be spared. He made a full confession of his guilt, thinking thereby to save his life. But all the means he resorted to were utterly useless. Die he must. It therefore became my duty to prepare him for his approaching fate. I read the Scriptures to him, especially the portions that relate to death, judgment, and eternity. I endeavoured to convince him that he was a sinner, both by nature and by practice; and then pointed him to the glorious remedy which God, in his infinite wisdom and mercy, has provided for the lost. He seemed affected and impressed with what I said; and in this frame of mind was urged by me to cast himself on the mercy of God in Christ.

I remained with him during the last four nights he was in the condemned cell in the Calton Hill Jail. During the first three I had some hope of his conversion. On the fourth night he became quite frenzied, and got up in the middle of the night, and demanded a knife. I unfortunately happened to have one in my pocket; but I said to him, Do you think that I would bring a knife into

the prison ? Nothing, however, would satisfy him
but a knife, which he continued to demand furi-
ously. I entreated him to lie down, and spoke
kindly to him in order to compose his mind ; but
he still stood before me with clenched fists, as if
he intended to knock me down. He was a big,
strong, rough man, and I appeared as nothing in
his eyes. This was the hour of my extremity. I
was completely shut up to the Lord himself. In
this situation, and with hand held up to guard my
head, and with my eyes open, I prayed earnestly,
and with a loud voice to the Lord. My prayer
was heard, and in a short time the prisoner became
quiet as a lamb, and lay down. After so much
excitement, in a close cell, I felt greatly exhausted,
and said to Gilchrist that I must have the door
opened, but said this in such a way as would not
lead him to suppose I was afraid of him. Accordingly I called on the turnkey to open the
door, but he did not hear me the first time, on
which the prisoner said, " He 'll no hear ye." I
replied, " I will make him hear me," and called a
second time much louder. The turnkey heard
me, and shouted out in reply, " What do you
want ?" I said, " Come and see ;" on which he
came and opened the iron gate. I told him I
could not remain unless he allowed the door to
remain open. He did so. At the same moment,
rising up, I put the knife into his hand and
squeezed it, without speaking a word, as much as
to say, " Don't speak !" He understood me perfectly, and carried the knife away. Then my mind

became relieved. After the turnkey left us, I used
every means to compose his mind, and urged him
to engage in prayer. He commenced and said
some words, but never used the name of Jesus.
I told him that unless his petitions were presented
in the name of the Lord Jesus, they could neither
be heard nor answered. He replied, that he could
not pray, and felt as awkward in making the
attempt, as an inexperienced tradesman would
feel in trying to do the work of a clever mechanic.
Consequently I had to put words in his mouth.
I told him to confess his guilt over the finished
work of Christ, and to beg for pardon through
the blood of Jesus ; for without the shedding of
blood there was no remission. I farther said to
him, that Christ satisfied by his death the demands
of law and justice, and that his blood, when applied by the Spirit, pacified the conscience, and
reconciled the soul to God ; and to explain to
him the necessity of using the name of Jesus in
his prayers, I employed the following illustration,
which he, as he was a business man, could easily
understand :—

Suppose, said I, you wished to draw some
money out of the bank in which you had de-
posited your wealth ; if you forget to put your
signature at the bottom of the bill, the banker
will refuse to cash it when it is presented to him.
But if your name be attached to the bill, the
banker accepts it without hesitation. Just so with
our prayers ; they must be presented in his name,
and they will be answered for his sake.

In this way we spent the night. When morning came I went home full of gratitude to the Lord for sparing my life. As soon as I was under my own roof, I poured out my heart in praise to God, my wife joining with me, for his merciful interposition on my behalf. After prayer we sung the 124th Psalm, as one most appropriate to our circumstances at this time.

> " Had not the Lord been on our side,
>    May Israel now say ;
> Had not the Lord been on our side,
>    When men rose us to slay ;
> They had us swallowed quick."

In the evening I paid him another visit, and went with him, at the request of Mr Rose, from the Jail to the Lock-up. We were alone in the coach together. The prisoner's legs were chained to prevent his escape, but he had the use of his hands and arms. The anguish of his mind at this time was very great. He placed himself as far back as possible in the coach—which was driven quickly through the streets—lest he should be recognised by any of his acquaintances. His grief seemed to me to proceed from pride rather than from contrition. On reaching the Lock-up, I engaged with him in prayer, that his mind might be reconciled to the fate which awaited him, and afterwards requested him to lie down on his bed, and endeavour to obtain some sleep. He accordingly lay down, but not to sleep, for he spent a most restless and uneasy night. During the night he requested me to write to his wife. I refused, suspecting he designed to do me some harm, and that he wished to endeavour to make his escape. When I told him to write himself, he said he could not, as his mind was too agitated and confused to allow him to do it. At length he consented, on condition that I would dictate to him. I complied with his request, and he began to write his letter. As he proceeded, he heard the sound of the workmen's hammers engaged in erecting the scaffold. " Do you hear that ? " he said, " what shall I say now ? " I replied, " Tell your wife your feelings on hearing the sound of the preparations for your death." He did so. After this he sent for the turnkey of the Lock-up to learn if any one who had been hanged ever came to life again ; and the turnkey gave him some little encouragement. This led him to hope that he might yet bid defiance to death, who was to him, indeed, the king of terrors ; and so he made preparations for the better accomplishment of his purpose.

When dressing for the last time, he put on a pair of carpet shoes, to be light when hanging. He made his friends engage a doctor to bleed him as soon as his body should be taken down, and a cart to convey home his body with all possible speed. But he was cherishing a delusive hope. He was holding on by a slender thread. I told him he was a heavy man, and was sure to die, and urged him to prepare to meet his God in judgment.

Soon after this the authorities arrived, and ordered him to be brought before them. The turn-

key was obliged to drag him forward, so unwilling
was he to meet his fate. When brought before
those entrusted with the execution of his sentence,
Mr Porteous, the chaplain of the jail, addressed a
few words to him, and then engaged in prayer.
After this, he was asked if it was true that he had
murdered his first wife, when he roughly answered
"No." All being now ready for carrying the last
sentence of the law into effect, the prisoner asked
permission to retire to a private room on a certain
pretext. He there made another attempt to commit suicide, but failed. He saw now that there
was no escape ; but as he had learned from the
keeper that if the rope were adjusted in a particular way, the neck-bone would not be dislocated,
he begged the executioner to place it so. This, he
thought, would give him a chance after all. The
executioner complied with his request, and thus
verified the remark of an old writer, "that there
is mercy with the executioner, but none with the
devil." In a few moments after, the unfortunate
man was launched into eternity, notwithstanding
all his precautions to save his life.

I now come to relate the closing scene in the
lives of two men whom I had frequent opportunities of visiting whilst they lay under sentence of
death in the Calton jail. They had committed
murder. One of them was named Gow—the other
Beveridge. The former was a shoemaker—the
latter a blacksmith.

On returning home one evening, Gow found
his wife (who was given to "strong drink"), and

some of her drunken associates, tippling in his house. On attempting to turn them out, his wife ran to the stair-head, and called for the police, who instantly came, and, at the request of his wife, he was carried off to the police-office, where he lay all night. In the morning he went home, and, in a fit of passion, stabbed his wretched wife with a sharp knife, in consequence of which she died. Beveridge, like Gow, was a hard-working man, and had also a drunken wife. One morning, on coming in to breakfast, he found the fire out, no food prepared for him, the children all running naked about the house, and his wife drunk in bed, and unfit to do anything. He had often before seen his house in this deplorable condition, and at that time was so overcome with rage that he killed her at once.

These two men were apprehended, tried, found guilty, and sentenced to death, and were confined in the same cell. I had frequent opportunities of visiting them, and of conversing with them. Having by my sympathy and kindness gained their confidence, they listened to me with interest and attention. Gow opened his mind more freely than Beveridge, and seemed to have a tender heart and keen feelings. In proof of this, I may inform the reader that Gow, when a boy, had on one occasion harried a bird's nest; but perceiving that the female bird followed him, apparently lamenting her loss, he repented, and put back the nest in the spot from whence he had taken it. It was always a matter of the greatest wonder and astonishment to him how he ever could have had the heart to murder his wife. How it was that a man who had felt such pity for a poor little bird could experience none for the woman who was his wife, was to him a mystery he could not understand. To explain it, I unfolded to him the deceitful and desperately wicked character of the heart of man in its natural state. I tried to show how totally ignorant we were of the awful crimes we were capable of committing when unrestrained by the preventing grace of God, and exposed to temptation. I laboured to convince them of the heinousness of the crime of which they had been guilty. I pointed out the awful danger they were in, and the punishment that awaited them if they continued impenitent. The Holy Spirit seemed to give effect to my humble efforts to bring these two unhappy men to the "Friend of sinners." A great and striking change in their whole deportment and character soon became apparent. They seemed deeply humbled on account of their sins— anxiously sought salvation, through a crucified Redeemer—read the Bible—prayed fervently to God, and seemed to be reconciled to and at peace with God, through the death of his Son. The change on them was so striking, that, to my observation, they seemed like lambs.

How mysterious are the ways of God in bringing sinners to their right mind!

When conducted to the hall where the magistrates were waiting to receive them on the morning of execution, Mr Porteous addressed them, according to custom, and afterwards prayed. The unhappy criminals were then informed that somebody wanted them in an adjoining room. Gow suspected that the person who wanted them was the executioner. Instantly he fell upon his knees, and lifting up his hands, heart, and voice to God, prayed earnestly for mercy through the death and satisfaction of God's dear Son. Such a sight was, to me at least, most refreshing, and encouraged me to increased activity and diligence in endeavouring to bring sinners to God. In striving to do good to the souls of others, I have invariably benefited and done good to my own in the knowledge of God.

On the scaffold Gow addressed the magistrates, and requested them to change the law which empowered a woman to commit her husband to prison for the most trifling offence. The magistrates seemed to approve of what he said. In a few minutes both prisoners were in eternity.

I could narrate many similar cases; but not wishing to weary my readers, I shall only mention one more—viz., that of James Bell, a soldier in a cavalry regiment stationed at "Jock's Lodge," who shot the sergeant-major of the regiment, and for that crime was condemned to die. All Edinburgh sympathized with this man, on account of the peculiar circumstances which led him to commit the crime for which he was doomed to death. The sergeant-major, it appears, was a sour, ill-natured man. He was always ready to find fault, and punish severely for the smallest breach of discipline. I have heard that, when on the march, if he saw any of the men following not exactly in their proper place, he would order them to dismount, and carry their saddles by their horses' side. In consequence of this severity, he was hated by the men, and a number of them plotted to despatch him. For this purpose they agreed to cast lots, and he upon whom the lot should fall was to do the deed. The lot fell upon Bell, who embraced the first opportunity that presented itself, and shot the sergeant-major. For this most rash and sinful act, he was condemned to die. Whilst awaiting the execution of his sentence in the jail, he was visited by Dr Hunter, of the Tron Church, Edinburgh, who, I believe, was honoured of the Lord to effect his conversion. I myself had an opportunity of visiting him repeatedly during his imprisonment; and from all I saw and heard on these occasions, I believe him to have been a true penitent. During his confinement he had learned to read and pray, and much of his time seemed given to these exercises, of which he appeared very fond. Bell belonged to the Episcopal church, and Mr (now Bishop) Terrot, a minister of that church, came frequently to converse with him. On one occasion, I heard, with great pleasure and satisfaction, Dr Hunter relate to Mr Terrot the method he had employed in dealing with the prisoner on the concerns of his soul. He first laboured to convince him of his original guilt—there the root of the evil lay—that was the source of all the sin he had ever committed, and, in order that the stream might be pure, it was absolutely necessary that the fountain should be cleansed. This sin was sufficient to render a man guilty in the sight of God. But when a life of actual transgressions, and of daring rebellion against God, is added to the account, how awful must the condition of the sinner be, standing accused, as he does, by the holy law of God, and exposed to his just displeasure !

The man saw his lost and perishing condition, and was thus, as it were, constrained to look around him for succour and for safety. Christ was then presented to the awakened and penitent criminal, and he gladly embraced the Saviour.

I continued with him in the Lock-up during the whole of the last night he spent on earth. He slept comfortably until about three o'clock in the morning. He seemed perfectly composed, and well resigned to his fate. Before he had risen from his bed I engaged with him in prayer, and afterwards assisted him to put on his clothes. We went arm in arm to the scaffold, and as we came up the narrow passage leading to the fatal spot, the excitement was great. Many of the spectators wept, and all seemed to feel deeply for the stately soldier, as he marched with a firm and steady step to the scene of his last sufferings. He wept much, and held down his head all the way. The executioner was inexperienced, and blundered his business, and the people became enraged in consequence, and made great commotion. On observing the movement in the crowd, the unfortunate prisoner raised his hands, as much as to say, "Peace, be still—weep not for me—all is well!" At this moment I called out "Never mind these men—look up to Jesus. He is waiting to receive you!" Casting one look upwards, he made the fatal signal for the executioner to perform his duty, and in a few moments all was over!

.    .    .    .    .    .    .    .

I may remark that my persecutions and sufferings from the magistrates and policemen of Edinburgh, whilst I preached in the street, would be deemed almost incredible, were I fully to relate them. The latter being mostly Irishmen and Roman Catholics, did not sympathize with me. In all my preachings I considered it an important part of my duty to expose error and heresy, as well as to proclaim the " truth as it is in Jesus." And this procedure on my part raised me up many enemies and opponents. Papists, Unitarians, Morrisonians, and such like, were my bitter gainsayers. The theories of their leading men I attacked and refuted from the Scriptures. I spared none who held opinions that robbed God of his glory, and Christ of the dignity of his person and the efficacy of his work. The adversaries of truth tried every means they could think of to deter me from performing the work God had given me to do, but in vain. Their opposition only made me bolder in the cause of my blessed Master. I had "counted the cost," and was determined to "follow" him through "evil" as well as through "good report." I was stoned, imprisoned, and otherwise maltreated, but God stood near and protected me. With Paul, who said that he had fought with beasts at Ephesus, I might well say that I had fought with beasts in the streets of Edinburgh.

Compassion to the souls of men drove me to the streets and lanes of my native city, to plead with sinners, and persuade them to come to Jesus. The love of Christ constrained me to face all opposition in the performance of this great and glorious work. I was grieved to see multitudes thronging the "broad road" that leads to destruction, whilst I myself was in the enjoyment of a good hope through grace. In my preaching I dwelt much upon death and its consequences, the everlasting punishment that awaited ungodly and impenitent sinners, and the everlasting weight of glory that was laid up for the righteous.

Many a time the magistrates imprisoned me, but my wife always succeeded in getting me out of their hands. At last they determined to keep me in prison unless some respectable person would become bail for me to the amount of £2. In this manner they attempted to close my mouth, and prevent me from preaching the Gospel. I determined, however, to allow no man to risk his property for me, whatever might be the consequences, for I was resolved to preach the Gospel fully to all who came within the reach of my voice. When prevented from preaching in the streets of Edinburgh, I was like a bottle filled with new wine, ready to "burst," which must get vent in some way or other. So I made up my mind to go to the Links. There I stationed myself on a wall by the wayside. Many of those who resorted thither for amusement, as well as for the purpose of drying and bleaching clothes, assembled to hear me, and the Lord gave me great liberty in declaring his word to perishing sinners. The work was the Lord's, and he strengthened me to perform it. The late Dr Simpson, of the Tron Church, was the only minister at that time who encouraged me in my labours. He came forward before the multitudes that stood around me, and shook me by the hand, at the same time wishing me "God speed!" He approved of the doctrines which I taught. Shortly afterwards he came to hear me, and brought Mrs Simpson along with him. At the conclusion of the service, the little girl that accompanied them came up and presented me with some money, which I returned, saying I did not preach for money—I came not to seek theirs, but them.

Under my preaching, at this time, an accomplished lady was awakened to a sense of her danger and sinful condition, both by nature and practice. She called upon me frequently afterwards, that I might pray for her. I requested her to pray likewise, and she complied. Her earnestness, simplicity, and scripturalness of expression, perfectly astonished me. After obtaining peace with God through the blood of the Cross, she collected numbers of other young ladies together, and held prayer-meetings in her own house, and invited me to conduct the devotional exercises. Having become zealous for the promotion of Christ's cause, she obtained admission to the cells of the female prisoners in the jail, and a blessing attended her efforts to do good. Since then she has departed this life, and is now, I trust, through " faith and patience inheriting the promises."

---

Thus abruptly closes Robert Flockhart's autobiography. We might regret that he had not been spared to continue his history down to the period when he retired from active labour ; but while God disposed otherwise, our regrets are the less, since, in consequence of the kindness of the Rev. Mr Robertson of Newington, we can supply the reader with some very interesting reminiscences of our Street-Preacher, and his remarkable sayings. From the time to which he has brought down his biography, to the period of his death, there is a blank of many years. During these, he continued to preach in season and out of season. He was to be found every week-day evening at his post at the west-end of St Giles' Cathedral, and on the Sabbath evenings in front of the Theatre. The weather was all one to him—in frost, in snow, in rain, as well as in sweet summer eve, he might be seen about nine o'clock slowly wending his way to his post ; the good old

Gospel Mission is a non-profit organization dedicated to spreading the Gospel of Christ at the lowest possible cost to our customers. Send for our FREE catalog.

Name _____

Address _____

City, State, Zip _____

Gospel Mission, Box 318, Choteau, MT 59422

man in winter carrying a small lantern in his hand, and some kind friend behind him with the chair on which he stood. He began by singing a few verses of a psalm; this had the effect of arresting attention, and at length of gathering an audience. With the crowd around him, composed chiefly of outcasts, I have occasionally mingled. It was a sight to move any one, to see that grey old shattered man pouring forth his soul in prayer to God, or making appeals to the people of great power and tenderness. The age that cools men's passions had not cooled his zeal; his spirit rose above the weakness of the worn-out frame, and when he was tottering on the grave, it might be said of him, in regard to his inner life, " that his eye was not dim, neither was his natural strength abated." Two years after he was laid aside from his beloved work of preaching Christ to the lost, and before he had time to finish his autobiography, he was called to his rest. Edinburgh did itself honour in awarding him a sort of public funeral, of which the following account is extracted from the *Daily Express* :—

"A large company assembled at 7 Richmond Place, to follow the remains of this veteran street-preacher to the tomb. After religious services, conducted by the Rev. David Guthrie, the procession moved off at four o'clock, in the following order—Four baton-men, the soldiers of the various recruiting parties in the city, four abreast, by whom the coffin was borne shoulder-high; Mr James Flockhart, Dumbarton, brother of the deceased, and other relatives, accompanied by about 250 citizens of every rank, among whom were several members of Town Council, and ministers of various denominations. On the top of the coffin were placed the family Bible belonging to the deceased, and the hymn-book used by him for many years in his open-air exhortations. The procession proceeded to the Grange Cemetery, where the interment took place, and along the whole road passed between lines of men, women, and children, who had gathered to express their sympathy with the mournful proceedings."

# Reminiscences

---

NEWINGTON, *9th December* 1857.

MY DEAR DR GUTHRIE—In yielding to the wish you
have so kindly urged, that I should record some reminiscences of Robert Flockhart, I feel afraid, from the paucity of
my materials, that they can contribute but little to your
information, or to the illustration of his character. Still,
the very gleanings of the life of such a man are surely worth
preserving.

My acquaintance with him had only begun when he was
led in from active scenes to the chamber of solitude and
the bed of languishing. About two years elapsed between
that period and his death—two years during which (as he
he used to say) " he dwelt in his own hired house, receiving
all that came unto him, and teaching those things which
concern the Lord Jesus, with all confidence, no man for-
bidding him." Often, in the midst of my work, did I drop
in upon him, to be refreshed and quickened by the testi-
monies he was wont to bear to the supports of God's grace
and the help of God's countenance; and never did I leave
him without feeling that I had learned, or ought to have
learned, the duty and happiness of living more as a pil-
grim-stranger, in habitual anticipation of the Bridegroom's
voice.

The peculiar pithy quaintness of his conversation, it is
difficult to convey a clear idea of by any description. Any
of his remarks, as written, must be greatly wanting in the

point they had when spoken in connection with the circumstances that produced them. His own *vernacularisms* you will probably approve of my seeking, as far as possible, to preserve.

Among those qualities which seemed to me to constitute his genuine worth were—

I. *His great delight in the Bible.*—While thankful for the sympathy of Christian friends, he uniformly declared that, " Had it not been for the companionship of God's word, its light and consolation," he " would have perished in his affliction." " I have just been sitting," he would say, " under its shadow with great delight, and finding its fruit sweet to my taste. There are grand, sweet apples on that tree. There's the apple of justification—'justified freely by his grace.' There's the apple of sanctification—' we are made partakers of his holiness.' There's the apple of adoption—' Now are we the sons of God.' And, best of all, there's the golden apple of glorification—we'll get that by and by; but 'it doth not yet appear what we shall be.' I mind when I've been in tropical countries, I've seen trees whose fruit just seemed as if it wanted to drop into your mouth, it was so rich and ripe. And doesn't the Lord say to us, when we come to this blessed book, Now, ' open thy mouth wide and I will fill it.' "

One day, as he sat looking into the fire, he said to me, " I was thinking about that verse, ' Is not my word as a fire and as a hammer?' saith the Lord. Ay, both a fire and a hammer; the one would not do without the other. I would not have been here if his word had not been a fire; my 'will' was such an 'iron sinew' in my unconverted state. But the Lord put my iron will into his fire to make it bend; it was a fire of fierce convictions. I believe my fire was heated seven times hotter than ordinary. But even that by itself would not answer the purpose of making me into ' a vessel meet for the master's use.' When the iron came out of the fire, He took to the hammer. It was none o' your wee hammers ; it was the Lord's sledge-hammer. You've seen a smith when he was working at the fore-hammer, how he tuckt up his sleeve ? Well, ' the Lord made bare his holy arm' in order to do his own work on me ; and it was a' needed—a' needed."

While noticing his love for the Bible, I may advert to the sort of instinctive dexterity with which he made the most simple incident subservient to the enforcement of Bible truth. For instance, speaking of the time when he first saw the sin-bearing Saviour, he said to me, " Well, you know, after that how I wondered that all the world did not see him too. I fell to telling all my comrades what a Saviour I had found ; and there was one o' them, a young lad—Edward Brown—that I took great pains to instruct in the ways of peace ; but he was little the better of my concern about his soul, for he soon ran again into excess of riot. He was taken up on charge of having to do with a highway robbery, and along with two other soldiers, was condemned to be hanged. The night before the execution, he sent for me, and said, ' You've been very kind to me, Flockhart ; I want to make you my heir ; to leave you all my effects.' So the morning came, when we were all ordered out to attend the execution. There were the three with the halters round their necks. I had heard o' ' mercy at the foot o' the ladder,' but I never saw it till then. For almost at the last minute a message came that there was a pardon for Edward Brown. " Well, lad," says I to myself, " you've got your life, but I've lost my legacy ; for ' a testament is of no force while the testator liveth.' But" (turning to me with a beaming face), he added, " Isn't it precious that we're so sure that Jesus died ; it is attested by so many ' infallible proofs.' ' He died for our sins according to the Scriptures.' We need not fear about losing our legacy because there's any doubt about the reality of his death. But we may fear something else. My wife had once a legacy left her by a lady. The lady was dead, beyond a doubt, but the lawyers got the legacy into their hands, and it was not easy, I assure you, gettin't out again. In fact, they wasted it among them, and my wife never saw a sixpence o't. Had the kind lady been living, she would have had the business better managed. And isn't it doubly precious to know that our Redeemer liveth?' ' He liveth by the power of God.' He has made himself responsible to be the executor of his own will. When we put our case into his hands, he'll let none wrong us o' our legacy."

At another time, speaking of the risen Redeemer meeting his disciples on the shore of the sea of Tiberias, he observed, " I suppose the kind salutation to them, ' Children, have ye any meat?' had a higher aim than the supply of their bodily wants. Ay, something was to be set right wi' Peter that day, and the plan Jesus took was wonderful like himself. He knew that the seafaring trade is a hungry trade ; so, in order to keep Peter's temper sweet, he had a refreshment ready for him. And it was only after the meal was ended (' when they had dined') that he turned to him and asked, ' Simon, son of Jonas, lovest thou me?' He did not cut him short and say, ' You denied me the other day, Sir.' No, he took a more telling way of his own. The three ask-ings would put Peter in mind of how often he had misbe-haved in the high priest's hall before the cock crowed outside ; and maybe the very ' fire of coals' on the shore might be just a picture of the fire at which he had warmed himself that cold night when the breath of a woman threw him down."

This " maybe it might be a picture" struck me as not a little remarkable as coming from one who had no knowledge of the Greek original, and as confirmed by the fact that there is only one other place in the New Testament where the Greek word translated "fire of coals" is found. It is where this same Evangelist John is relating what took place "that cold night" in the palace of the high priest. Does it not indeed give emphasis to the "maybe," that busy memory may have been carrying Peter back to the very scene, and that there may have come thronging up before him, now the strong glare of that fire, the taunting questions of the silly maid, and the piercing look of Jesus—now when he sees, on the wild sea-shore, lighted up mysteriously, miraculously, just such another "fire of coals."

II. Robert Flockhart was *eminently a man of prayer*.—On no point, perhaps, did I hear him speak oftener than on the sinfulness of "restraining prayer,"—the weight of guilt lying in these days on the churches of Christ, and on individual Christians, for spending in idle visits, frivolous talk, and unprofitable reading, time that might be redeemed for prayer. One evening (and I believe it was one of the last on which he was able to take his accustomed place on the street) I happened to call upon him about an hour before his usual preaching hour. On reaching his door I found the room dark; but remaining quite still, I could overhear him, in a deep under-tone, "as a man talketh with his friend," telling out to the Lord his griefs and fears, his designs and expectations, in regard to the work he was going to—"Lord, dinna forsake Edinburgh! dinna forsake Edinburgh! Why should our preaching here be so powerless? Consciences are not pricked, hearts are not broken, souls are not saved. The enemy is come in as a flood. Oh, pluck thy right hand out of thy bosom! Lord, dinna forsake Edinburgh!"

It was real pleading, real wrestling, "crying out of the depths." When he ceased, and I had stepped forward, he rekindled his light, and as soon as he recognised me, exclaimed, "O, I'm glad it's you, for we'll be of one mind on

the matter.   You know 'we must give ourselves continually
to prayer and to the ministry of the word.'   Prayer is the
one half of our work, the first half, and the best half too.
Oh! what poor weak things we would be if we were not
made 'mighty through God.'"   Thus did the good old man
string his soul for active service by living near the Throne.
Thus did he go to his post on the street, strong in the
power of prayer.

At whatever time I called upon him, I never got away
without our praying together, the one following the other.
"I hope you're not in a hurry," he would say ; "we cannot
leave out 'agreeing together' to entreat the Lord.   Maybe
we'll never meet on praying ground again."

He carried everything that interested him to the mercy-
seat, and he had strong faith in the efficacy of prayer.   These
were among his favourite maxims—that we are "sure to
get relief if we go direct to Christ for it," and that we should
set our hearts not only to "desire greater things than we
have gotten yet, but to be aye on the look-out for them."

I have it on the testimony of one who waited on him
much during the closing years of his life, that when alone
he spent almost all his time in prayer.   Every morning at
seven he commenced domestic worship.   When afraid, at
certain times, of not being awake by that time, he would
arrange with the baker to come precisely at the honr.   On
the Fridays he got in his week's provision, that he might
not be disturbed on the Saturday, this being a day he set
apart for meditation and special intercession for a blessing
on the Sabbath and the labours of the ministry.

He was peculiarly fond of praise-singing, and frequently
expressed his astonishment that Christian people should
leave praise out of their family-worship, especially since
they professed to expect that praise would be their employment for ever in glory.   He sometimes alluded to the fact,
that when he was first married, he and his wife lived for a

time in the same house with a family that had no objections to his making worship; " only," said he, " they would not let me sing, for fear, I suppose, the neighbours would know what we were at from the sound. Weel, I reasoned with them, and would not give in. All the baits by which they tried to put me past it, I rejected. So at last, says I to my wife, ' Annie, this will never do. We maun hae a house o' our ain.' And so we got one, and it was a Bethel to us, where there was ' heard the voice of joy and melody.' Oh ! it is pleasant, and to praise, ' it is a comely thing.' "

When talking of his wife, at another time, he said, " I had one of the best of wives. We were just like two ponies in a chariot, we pulled so well together. We began our acquaintance with prayer, and we continued with one accord in prayer and supplication for nine-and-twenty years. When we first met, and I told her my errand, ' Well,' she says, ' my wish has been, if I did not get a praying man, never to get any.' And my answer was, ' The thing is surely of the Lord; let us acknowledge him in prayer together before we go farther.' A few days after somebody said to her, ' You're such a fool to take a sodger.' So she sent me word that she had ta'en the rue. Shortly after that, I went to see her, and said, ' What ails you now, Annie ?' She made several excuses, and I only said, ' Then I'll hae to gang hame and pray for you.' The next night she sent me word that ' all was right again.' So I got her."

Sometime after their marriage, his wife and he went to visit his father and mother at Old Kilpatrick. " The first night we arrived," said he, " as it drew towards bed-time, I asked, ' You're going to take the books (Bibles for family-worship), arn't ye ?' Father and mother both held down their heads. Says I, ' I cannot stay here unless you make worship. I doubt I'll have to go somewhere else.' ' Robie,' said my wife, ' dinna speak that way.' My mother, poor body, and my wife both, fell a-crying. Then they said, 'You'll just take the books yourself, Robie." 'No, no, says I, 'it maun be the head of the house; that's his duty.' 'Robie,' said my father to me, 'I cannot pray.' 'Well,' says I, 'just tell the Lord that, and that'll do to begin wi'.'"

"For all this," he added, "I dearly loved my father and mother. 'My heart's desire was, that they might be saved.' The next year, when we went back to see them, we had a happy meeting, for now they had worship regularly, and the father could pray far better than the son."

His prayers were marked by an affectionate precision. Every Christian friend, and every object of Christian interest, were sure of a warm and special mention. He was emphatically one of those who "sigh and cry for the sins of the land." He had "great heaviness and continual sorrow of heart for his brethren, his kinsmen according to the flesh." He made the burden of a dying world his own. I am told by one who was much with him, that during all the time of the Crimean war, he spent some portion of every day in interceding for the soldiers, and that, when he heard of their doing any brave thing, the old martial spirit used to be stirred within him. He would laugh and rub his hands, and say, "Shouldn't it just be the same wi' Christ's sodgers? They must charge on the enemy; not content wi' aye pop, poppin wi' the rifles. That's no the way to do. But up and into the heart o' them! Three cheers, and down wi' the enemy's colours! That's the way to carry the day."

He took much pleasure in talking of "the church in the army" in India—"how prayerful they were," and "how warm their love was to each other." He was wont to say, "Christian love in this country is like Greenland to theirs." He had a strong affection for all who love the Lord and whom the Lord loves, to whatever denomination they belonged, if he felt persuaded of their consistent adherence to the grand distinctive doctrines of grace, though on this point he was well known to be "jealous with a godly jealousy." When I was leaving him one afternoon, a young man came in, as if from College, with books in his hand. He turned to me, and said in a whisper, "That's a gracious student. I know you like to see a gracious student." He gathered round him regularly, I understand, a number of such students for the purposes of social devotion, and these scenes were felt to be like a hallowed mount, from which they came down again to the world, prepared to be less ruffled by its cares, and less vulnerable by its temptations. Several times I took Christian friends along with me to see him, and often afterwards did they refer to such visits as seasons of peculiar refreshment and quickening. By the light he cast on Scripture texts, and his fixed earnestness of soul in pleading the promises, they learned better how to "fight the good fight of faith," through strength derived from God.

III. The only other distinguishing feature of his character I shall notice is his *zeal in seeking to win souls.* "When the Lord began a work of grace in my heart," said he, "I made a vow, that if he would spare me as long in his service as I had been in the service of the devil, I would do all in my power to try and bring as many souls to him, through the grace of his own Spirit, as I had been instrumental in destroying. I was a ringleader in all evil, a perfect Napoleon in Satan's ranks. So I have good reason to be greedy for the conversion of souls." Indeed, it was from the quiver of his own experience he ever drew his sharpest arrows. It seemed deeply fixed in his mind, and interwoven with all his convictions, that it was his calling —not his by-job, but his business—to go on a Saviour's errand in quest of lost souls—to seek to snatch them from perdition, like firebrands from the flame.

I have it on the testimony of a Christian friend who was

intimately conversant with all his habits, that "when going out to preach in the evening, he could not say a word unless he had first, for a considerable while, wrestled with the Lord for a blessing." And even at those times when he was scarcely able to walk to the place, " ere he was done with preaching he was strong as a lion." On getting home, he " stirred up the fire, and then immediately to his knees, to tell the Lord all about what had occurred on the street that night, and to beseech him to seal the word spoken by making it the means of conversion to somebody."

One night, when he had mounted his chair at St Giles', and was about to commence his work, as usual, by singing praise, a woman stepped forward and said, " Mr Flockhart, you'll never attempt to preach in sic a nicht as this," for it rained very heavily. " Whisht, woman ! " he replied, "and be thankful that the Lord's not raining down fire and brimstone on you and me out o' heaven." The woman was startled, and said no more. " So," to use the words of my informant, " Robbie set to work in earnest, determined not to be afraid of the elements."

Another night, when he was discoursing on the spirituality of the Law, and how God has threatened his fierce wrath against every one that goeth on in his iniquity, some passers-by came and listened for a little while, and then went away. But he lifted up his voice, and cried after them, " Ye're not fond, I see, o' the sparks fleeing about your ears. I doubt ye may be like the dog in the smith's shop when the red-hot iron is on the anvil. Just when the hammer is coming down, the dog, poor beast, runs in below the bench for fear. And is that the way wi' you ? "

This incident reminds me of one of the first remarks he made to me when I first met him. We were speaking of how difficult it is to awaken reflection and produce conviction in the minds of the ungodly, when he stated that he had almost always found the most alarming subjects the

most useful, and he added, " You never saw a woman
sewing without a needle ? She would come but poor speed
if she only sewed wi' the thread. So, I think, when we're
dealing wi' sinners, we maun aye put in the needle o' the law
first ; for the fact is, they're sleeping sound, and they need to
be wakened up wi' something sharp. But when we've got
the needle o' the law fairly in ; we may draw as lang a
thread as you like o' Gospel consolation after't."

Certainly, he was not one of those who, by their preaching, sew pillows under the arms of sleepy professors—
who " prophesy smooth things," and " heal hurts|slightly,"
and " cry, Peace, peace, when there is no peace." " I believe," said he, on one occasion, " though the High Street
were strewed with the blessings of God's grace, there's such
hard-heartedness and ungodliness among the folk here, they
would not stop to lift up one of the gifts so freely given
them of heaven. Oh ! they're a generation o' vipers, the
drunken, scoffing crew ! They fasten like vipers on the
very hand of God. But if they dinna mend, I tell them
what God will do. He'll shake the vipers off his hand into
the fire, the devouring fire, the unquenchable fire, and yet
he'll ' feel no harm.' "

Speaking of those that are " backsliders in heart," he observed, " When the fire of grace is burning low in our
hearts, it's high time to be clearing out the ribs, and the
first way to do that is by making free confession. ' I said,
I will confess,' and I no sooner ' said it,'—I no sooner began
to ' muse,'—than ' the fire' began to ' burn.' ' I said I will
confess my transgression unto the Lord, and thou forgavest
the iniquity of my sin.'"

" Yes," continued he, with a peculiar arch look, " It is
' unto the Lord' we're to make our confession, and not, like
the papists, to a creature like ourselves. I tell these Catholics often that they ' worship they know not what.' They
not only worship saints, but they worship sinners. For they

say prayers to the Virgin Mary, and was she not a sinner? Ask herself, and she'll tell you. 'My spirit doth rejoice in God my Saviour.' Yes, she confesses that she needed a Saviour. What need could she have for a Saviour if she was not a sinner? Yet they worship her. Can folk be in their senses that worship that way?"

He was a fearless assailant of all popish mummeries and corrupt abominations, and often on the street he had a preaching crusade against them. One night, about the time that Pio Nono fled from Rome, he addressed the Roman Catholics around him thus:—"What will ye do now without your Pope! He has run awa, the coward! No doubt he is an 'hireling,' for 'he leaveth the sheep.' You'll surely never call him your shepherd any more after this. It is the shepherd's duty (isn't it?) to stand by the sheep 'when the wolf cometh;' but instead o' that, your shepherd sends to France and hires sodgers to shoot the sheep."

"The Lord's my shepherd, I'll not want." Whoever o' you can say that from the heart, all the promises o' that bonnie 23d Psalm are yours. Your shepherd is the good Shepherd, who 'laid down his life for you,' and 'none shall be able to pluck you out of his hand."

In the course of another night's work he had occasion to speak of Socinians, and referring to what he had heard about the sinking of the ground beneath the walls of the Socinian Chapel, he uttered warning words to this effect:— "It's plain that it is a sinking concern a'thegether. The system's built upon the sand. Any body that is taking shelter there had 'better escape for his life.' For, 'when the rains descend, and the floods come, and the winds blow, the ruin of that house will be great.'" Indeed all the sophistries of the "wise and prudent," which seemed to him to becloud "the truth as it is in Jesus," he held up before the pure, unflattering mirror of the Word, and then rebuked and denounced them with unsparing fidelity.

There is reason to believe that he endeavoured to conduct his street-work with as little interruption as possible to the free transit of passengers, yet the time was when (as he thought) there were unreasonable complainers, and some disposition to lend too ready an ear to their complaints, and to interpose authority when there was really no annoyance. Hence some of his characteristic sallies against what he deemed the wantonness of a wayward humour on the part of the police. For example, when enumerating, in his discourse one night, the singular trophies of grace that would be found in heaven, he exclaimed, "There are saved Manassehs in heaven, and saved Magdalenes in heaven, and saved Sauls in heaven, and saved publicans in heavens, and I believe it's possible that there may be saved policemen in heaven!"

It may be of some consequence to notice it as a practical hint, derived from his experience, that when he preached about nine o'clock at night, he could get a much larger assemblage of the very class he had in view than when he took any earlier hour. He felt more and more that if we wish to get hold of careless people we must "watch them and catch them at their idle time," and "become all things to all men," in order "to save some."

When he heard that the matter of open-air preaching was stirring so much the minds of ministers and churches, it made him very happy, and he said, "You will never get at the ignorant and the profligate mass without it. I'm so glad I had to bear the brunt o't for you. I had to 'suffer shame' many a day for what's so respectable now. I had to go to 'bonds and imprisonments' for doing what our Master did, for he preached far oftener by the road-side, and by the sea-side, than in the synagogue." Well did he know, and often testified how well he knew, that one great cause of the ill success of the gospel among the careless multitude is their disposition to regard stated official ministrations within church-walls as just so much paid work. But when one approaches them on whom they have no claim—one who asks nothing but a patient hearing, and who exposes himself to toil, and contempt, and danger, for no conceivable reason except that he is seeking to do them good,—in this case, a state of feeling is produced peculiarly fitted to gain attention, and, by the blessing of God, to ensure saving impression. How much better to die of George Whitfield's asthma, or of Robbie Flockhart's palsy, through " labours more abundant " in such service, than to die of dignity through letting it alone.

He was going on with his street-work with undiminished zeal when palsy overtook him. " We've met at last," said he, speaking of the disease, " and we'll never be parted but at the grave's mouth." For some days he seemed to be hovering between life and death, yet he rallied again with wonderful rapidity, though never to the reattaining of that point of strength from which this attack had brought him down. His wonted vivacity and cheerfulness still remained unshadowed. I never saw him spiritually depressed. He regarded it as his duty to " rejoice in the Lord always," as really as it is to " pray without ceasing." And upon this he was accustomed to lay particular stress, as the true way of honouring " the God of all comfort."

To adopt the expression of one of his friends, " He appeared to take that palsy as kindly from the Lord's hand as if some one had left him a fortune." Yet he did say at times, "I feel my wings are clipped now. I'm like a bird wi' a stone tied to its leg. It tries to get up, but cannot rise. The time's coming, though, when I'll be relieved o' this heavy load. Then I'll clap my glad wings and flee away. I'll be young again when I reach that happy home. How I'll make the arches o' heaven ring with loud hallelujahs to God and the Lamb for ever! Oh, what a glorious body 'the celestial body' will be! No blear-eyed Leahs nor limpin Jacobs up yonder!"

One of the last times I was with him, we were speaking of Christ's "learning obedience by the things which he suffered," when he said, "Ay, but what a difference there is between his language in his state of humiliation and in his state of exaltation. In his humiliation, it was 'Father, not my will, but thine be done.' But now, in his exalted state, he says, 'Father, I will.'" And he gets the request of his lips, when any believer dies, 'Father, I will that they whom thou hast given me be with me where I am, to behold my glory.'"

As his end drew near, his thoughts appeared to dwell the more delightedly on "the things that are above." For instance, one afternoon when heaven was the theme of our conversation, he remarked that "Faith, Hope, and Love will be our good company all the way up to the door o' our Father's house. But there Faith will make her bow, and retire, saying, 'You'll not need me more, for you're now to "see him as he is, without a veil." And Hope, too, will say, 'Farewell! I've been glad to get you guided this length. And now, when I've served your turn, I must see after other pilgrims coming the same road.' But Love will smile and say, 'You and I are not to part that way. No, no! I'm going in to stay wi' you to all eternity."

It needs but to be added, that he died as he had lived, to the praise of God's grace. It was striking and most instructive to witness how his long life of active service came in no degree into the account of his final hope. His heart, in the end, found rest alone in the merits of him who had been "the beginning of his confidence." And, with this sure anchor before him, he passed "within the veil."

My dear Dr. Guthrie,—Though my materials derived from intercourse with him are not exhausted, I feel afraid you may think I have forgotten the good maxim "ne quid nimis," so I bring these very hastily-written lines to a close. It is in deference to your own kind and repeated solicitation that I send them, being glad of any opportunity of testifying with what cordial esteem I am, yours very affectionately,

JAMES ROBERTSON.